T0316658

Cambridge Elements ≡

Elements in Corporate Governance
edited by
Thomas Clarke
Centre for Corporate Governance, UTS Business School

ASIAN CORPORATE GOVERNANCE

Trends and Challenges

Toru Yoshikawa
Singapore Management University

CAMBRIDGE
UNIVERSITY PRESS

CAMBRIDGE
UNIVERSITY PRESS

University Printing House, Cambridge CB2 8BS, United Kingdom

One Liberty Plaza, 20th Floor, New York, NY 10006, USA

477 Williamstown Road, Port Melbourne, VIC 3207, Australia

314–321, 3rd Floor, Plot 3, Splendor Forum, Jasola District Centre,
New Delhi – 110025, India

79 Anson Road, #06–04/06, Singapore 079906

Cambridge University Press is part of the University of Cambridge.

It furthers the University's mission by disseminating knowledge in the pursuit of
education, learning, and research at the highest international levels of excellence.

www.cambridge.org
Information on this title: www.cambridge.org/9781108450362
DOI: 10.1017/9781108552936

First published 2018

A catalogue record for this publication is available from the British Library.

ISBN 978-1-108-45036-2 Paperback
ISSN 2515-7175 (online)
ISSN 2515-7167 (print)

Asian Corporate Governance

Toru Yoshikawa

Singapore Management University

Abstract: *This Element aims to achieve three objectives. First, it explores some key institutional characteristics of several Asian economies that are relevant to corporate governance practices. Second, it reviews corporate governance codes or rules in those economies and examines levels of requirements in terms of formal rules. Third, this Element looks at recent trends related to corporate governance such as executive compensation and a proportion of independent directors on boards of large listed firms.*

Keywords: *corporate governance, Asia, corporate governance codes, board of directors, executive compensation*

ISSNs: 2515-7175 (online), 2515-7167 (print)
ISBNs: 9781108450362 PB, 9781108552936 OC

1 Introduction

Asian economies are heterogeneous in terms of, for example, level of economic development, political system, and national culture, and consequently the region has a variety of business systems and practices. Corporate governance system is no exception and each Asian economy has its own uniqueness. However, since the late 1990s especially after the Asian Financial Crisis, we can observe a trend that can be characterized by the adoption of some elements of Western, particularly the Anglo-American model of corporate governance. Because of this trend, there is some convergence in corporate governance practices among Asian economies (Yoshikawa & Rasheed, 2009). Corporate governance codes of many Asian economies call for the presence of independent directors on the corporate board and often require greater information disclosure than in the past. Yet, due to heterogeneity within the region, there are still country-specific characteristics that are reflected in corporate governance codes and how corporate governance is actually practiced in each economy.

This Element aims to achieve three objectives. First, it will review some key institutional characteristics of several Asian economies that are relevant to corporate governance practices. For example, ownership structure of listed firms varies greatly among Asian economies – from relatively dispersed ownership in large Japanese firms to more concentrated ownership by family or state owners in other Asian economies. Such differences would inevitably affect how corporate governance is actually practiced. Second, this Element will review corporate governance codes or rules in those economies and examine levels of requirements in terms of formal rules. Third, the Element will show some recent trends related to corporate governance such as executive compensation and proportion of independent directors on boards of large listed firms. These issues are summarized and compared at the discussion section at the end of the Element. This Element covers six Asian economies, i. e., Japan, Singapore, South Korea, China, Taiwan, and Malaysia. I chose those economies based on the size of economy as well as the level of economic development. Before I examine corporate governance in each economy, the next section briefly presents the recent states of corporate governance in these six economies.

2 Quality of Corporate Governance in Asia

Asian Corporate Governance Association has been issuing the rankings of corporate governance in Asia. Table 1 shows the rankings in 2016 based on the assessments using questionnaire on five different categories, i.e., corporate governance rules and practices, enforcement, political and regulatory environment, accounting and auditing, and corporate governance culture. What we can observe from these rankings is that the level of economic development appears to be related to the rankings with some exception

Table 1 Corporate Governance Rankings in Asia

%	Total	CG rules and practices	Market category scores (CG Watch 2016)			
			Enforcement	Political and regulatory	Accounting and auditing	CG culture
1 Singapore	67	63	63	67	87	55
2 Hong Kong	65	65	63	69	70	53
3 Japan	63	51	63	69	75	58
4 Taiwan	60	54	54	64	77	50
5 Thailand	58	64	51	45	77	42
6 Malaysia	56	54	54	48	77	50
7 India	55	59	51	56	58	49
8 Korea	52	48	50	53	70	41
9 China	43	38	40	36	67	34
10 Philippines	38	35	19	41	65	33
11 Indonesia	36	35	21	33	58	32

Source: Asian Corporate Governance Association

Table 2 Changes in Asian Corporate Governance Scores
(CG Watch)

	2007	2010	2012	2014	2016
Singapore	65	67	69	64	67
Japan	52	57	55	60	63
Taiwan	54	55	53	56	60
Malaysia	49	52	55	58	56
Korea	49	45	49	49	52
China	45	49	45	45	43

Source: Asian Corporate Governance Association

(i.e., Korea), but the size of economy does not seem to be a key factor although the top two in the rankings, Singapore and Hong Kong, are small economies.

If we look at the changes in the rankings (ranking scores) over time, as shown in Table 2, we can observe that some countries or economies such as Japan and Taiwan have been improving their corporate governance rankings while others are relatively stable. Singapore has consistently achieved high ranking scores while China has remained at lower scores.

Singapore is ranked first in Asia in 2016, and higher scores in 2016 compared to 2014 indicate its efforts to further improve the quality of its governance. Singapore has been competing with Hong Kong for the top position in Asia in the past decade and has been maintaining high corporate governance standards. Japan is ranked the third with higher scores compared to 2014 due to the new corporate governance rules (e.g., the new Corporate Governance Code). Japanese corporate governance has shown an upward trend since 2007, suggesting some concerted efforts, which I will discuss later. Taiwan's ranking scores have also improved due to strong political support and changes in governance rules. While Malaysia's score has been rather stagnant since 2012, Korea has shown some improvement from 2014. China remains in lower scores, and its rankings have not changed much since 2007 due to the lack of major corporate governance reforms. Compared to some other Asian economies that have been improving the quality of corporate governance, China's standards have been relatively declining although they are still higher than the Philippines and Indonesia (not shown in the table). Trends in these economies indicate that the government and regulatory bodies in each economy have exerted different degrees of efforts on improving corporate governance of companies listed on local stock exchanges. I will now examine each economy in detail.

3 Japan

3.1 Institutional Context

Like in many other countries, boards of directors of Japanese firms are legally responsible for managerial monitoring for important decision-makings. Japanese firms also have single-tier boards like US firms but unlike German boards where the supervisory board functions to monitor the management board under two-tier board structure. However, executives or company insiders have been dominating most Japanese boards for a long time. One of the key reasons for this practice is that a board position has often been treated as the highest position that employees can reach if they successfully win internal competition (Charkham, 1994). Another reason is that until recently there was no formal requirement to have independent outsides on the board in Japanese firms. Indeed, the number of outside directors, if any, on many Japanese boards has been small, and most of outside directors were not independent but rather affiliated with related parties such as banks, business partner firms such as suppliers, and parent firms, or ex-bureaucrats transferred from government agencies (Miwa & Ramseyer, 2005; Sheard, 1994). Outside directorships have usually been used to cement business relationships, and they were often sent by strategic shareholders (David et al., 2010; Gerlach, 1992) rather than being appointed as representatives of financial investors. Therefore, the Japanese board has been *de facto* top management team.

In terms of ownership structure, large portions of outstanding shares of listed Japanese firms have been owned by such strategic shareholders that are domestic banks and non-financial firms. Those shareholders are usually categorized as "stable" shareholders because they usually do not sell their shareholdings for financial gain (Ahmadjian & Robinson, 2001; Gerlach, 1992). Due to this ownership structure, hostile takeovers have been rare in Japan. Instead of capital market discipline, domestic banks have been playing an important monitoring role as many Japanese firms relied on bank finance, and banks with their shareholdings in their customer firms had significant influence over borrower firms (Aoki, Jackson, & Miyajima, 2007).

These features allowed Japanese executives not to pay much attention to investors who hold shares for financial return. Instead, Japanese firms tended to focus on growth, employment protection, and profits rather than stock performance (Ahmadjian & Robinson, 2001). Partly due to this ownership structure, Japanese corporate governance system is often perceived as stakeholder-oriented rather than shareholder-oriented (Aoki et al., 2007; Gedajlovic & Shapiro, 2002). Nevertheless, ownership concentration of listed Japanese firms have been steadily declining and the concentration ratio is much lower than that in many other developed economies (Crossland & Hambrick, 2011), especially in Europe where many firms still have large family ownership.

3.2   Initial Developments

Japanese corporate governance practices discussed above started to change from the late 1990s, especially after the financial regulatory changes. As Japanese banks were facing grave difficulty after the Asian Financial Crisis (e.g., some banks went bankrupt) and subsequent consolidation of major domestic banks, their role in corporate governance has declined substantially. Even though large Japanese firms had already started to use capital market financing before the 1990s, the banking crisis further weakened the bank-centered corporate governance system. Further, due to the accounting change that forced Japanese firms to use market value rather than book value of their shareholdings for accounting purposes, many firms started to decrease their shareholdings in other firms leading to declining shareholdings by domestic stable shareholders. As domestic shareholders reduced their shareholding positions, the presence of foreign institutional investors has become larger. Since foreign institutional investors hold shares to gain financial return through capital appreciation or dividend income, pressure on Japanese executives to pay greater attention to capital market performance started to rise.

From this period, a series of regulatory changes have been implemented, including the legalization of stock option compensation in 1997 and the legal change in 2004 to allow Japanese firms to adopt the "committee system" modeled after the US corporate governance model with three committees, i.e., audit, nomination, and compensation committees. While the number of firms that adopted stock option compensation has increased substantially (Geng, Yoshikawa, & Colpan, 2016), the committee system has not spread as much.

3.3 Recent Developments

In the last few years, Japan has undergone major reforms with the adoption of Stewardship Code in 2014 and the issuance of the corporate governance code that reflects the government's determination and commitment to help enhance firm performance. These initiatives stem from the lack of confidence in local practices including corporate governance to revitalize the sluggish domestic economy. After Prime Minister Abe took the power, he has been pushing for a series of reform initiatives to revitalize the Japanese economy, and the newly introduced corporate governance code by Tokyo Stock Exchange, which aimed to improve a managerial monitoring function of the board of directors by including independent directors, is one such initiative.

In addition, more Japanese firms are beginning to be more receptive to engaging investors, which is one of the trends supported by Stewardship Code. Due to the increasing trend of investors voting against management that are not performing at the satisfactory level, this has motivated institutional investors to find ways to improve their investment returns. This is evident from the nine companies in the TOPIX 500 where the CEO's re-election was approved by less than 80 percent in 2015, and their return on equity has improved by an average of 2.4 percent in 2016 (Ethical Boardroom, 2017). This is the first broad stock index that includes only profitable companies with good corporate governance. All these changes indicate that the ecosystem of Japan is gradually changing and becoming relatively more favorable for investors that seek higher returns.

3.4   Stewardship Code and Corporate Governance Code

As part of the Japan Revitalization Strategy first approved by the Cabinet in June 2013, the Tokyo Stock Exchange introduced a Stewardship Code and the Corporate Governance Code, in 2014 and 2015 respectively. The Stewardship Code aims to provide guiding principles for institutional investors to fulfill their stewardship responsibilities to clients, beneficiaries, and investee companies. The Corporate Governance Code, on the other hand, outlines guiding principles for listed companies that will promote accountability to the various stakeholders of the corporations. Together, both codes serve as "two wheels of a cart" that aims to promote a virtuous economic cycle toward long-term sustainable growth for the Japanese economy through better firm performance.

3.4.1   Stewardship Code

The Stewardship Code highlights various guidelines for different institutional investors (i.e., institutional investors as asset managers and institutional investors as asset owners) to fulfil their fiduciary duties. It is stipulated that acceptance of the Code must be publicly disclosed by investors on their website, along with disclosure of information as required by the principles of the Code. Investors are also to include policies of how their stewardship responsibilities are fulfilled as well as explanation if there is non-compliance of any of the principles. Companies are also expected to review the provided information while notifying the Financial Services Agency of their website used to disclose such information (Financial Services Agency, 2014). The Code adopts the "comply or explain" approach and thus is not mandated as legal requirement. However, this also provides the authority with flexibility to constantly update the Code in response to changing business environments as well as global standards.

3.4.2   Corporate Governance Code

The Corporate Governance Code is based on the OECD Principles of Corporate Governance, and its primary purpose is to stimulate healthy corporate entrepreneurship, support sustainable corporate growth, and increase corporate value over the mid- to long-term.

The Code adopts the principles-based approach and a "comply or explain" approach as in the case of the Stewardship Code. Thus, the principles are not legally binding. However, all listed companies are required to submit a Corporate Governance Report to the Tokyo Stock Exchange regarding their compliance to the Code and explanations on any non-compliance.

This has also allowed the JPX to come up with a new index known as the JPX-Nikkei Index 400 introduced in January 6, 2014. This index is composed of companies that meet the requirement of global investment standards, such as the efficient use of capital and investor-focused management perspectives, and therefore they represent attractive investment targets for investors (Tokyo Stock Exchange, 2015).

3.5   *Specific Legal and Regulatory Changes*

In addition to the introduction of the Corporate Governance Code in 2015, Companies Reform Act was introduced in 2014. A series of reform initiatives entail the following key changes.
1) Appointment of outside directors
   Toky Stock Exchange has amended its listing rules whereby listed companies are required to appoint at least two independent outsiders as a director, which is different from an "outside

director." Beyond being an outside director as outlined in the Companies Act, these directors must not have any conflict of interest with management and the company.

2) New requirements on outside directors (or outside statutory auditors)

    a. No longer permit, among others, directors or employees of a parent company, management officers of affiliate companies, and certain close family members or relatives of a director of a company to serve as outside officers.

    b. Exceptions to allow person who has not served in the capacity of a management officer in the last 10 years to serve as an outside director of such company.

3) Introduction of an entirely new corporate governance system

    Introduction of a third corporate governance structure called a supervisory committee (on top of the traditional Kansayaku or statutory auditor system and the Committee System introduced in 2004), consisting of three or more directors of which at least a majority must be outside directors. This system aims to reduce the burden on companies to look for independent directors to serve on their board as well as on their auditing committees, as it is often suggested that the pool of qualified outside directors is still small in Japan.

3.6   Board Structure of Listed Firms

Based on the new rules, outside directors are deemed independent only when non-business relationship is established by each company. Otherwise, outside directors may be related to individuals who may be dealing heavily with the companies or related to companies that deal heavily with the board on which the director sits. Audit and Supervisory Board is independent from the board of directors and are tasked to work with the company's accounting and internal auditors. Following the introduction of such rules, the number of independent directors has indeed increased. Table 3 shows the board of director structure and the statutory audit board structure of the largest 20 firms on the

Table 3 Board Structure of the Largest 20 Firms in Japan (by Market Capitalization)

	Board of directors			Statutory audit board		
	Total	Outside	Outside + ID	Total	Outside	Outside + ID
Toyota Motor Corporation	11	3	3	6	3	3
NTT DOCOMO, Inc.	15	2	2	5	4	2
Mitsubishi UFJ Financial Group, Inc.*	17	7	7			
SoftBank Group Corp.	7	2	2	5	4	4
KDDI Corporation	14	5	3	5	3	3
Nippon Telegraph and Telephone Corporation	12	2	2	5	3	3
Japan Post Bank Co., Ltd.*	12	8	7			
Honda Motor Co., Ltd.	13	2	2	5	3	3
Sumitomo Mitsui Financial Group, Inc.*	14	5	5			
Mizuho Financial Group, Inc.*	13	6	6			
Keyence Corporation	10	2	2	3	3	3
Japan Tobacco Inc.	7	2	2	4	2	2
Nissan Motor Co., Ltd.	9	1	1	4	3	3
Fanuc Corporation	13	3	3	5	3	3

Table 3 (cont.)

	Board of directors			Statutory audit board		
	Total	Outside	Outside + ID	Total	Outside	Outside + ID
Sony Corporation*	11	8	8			
Canon Inc.	7	2	2	5	3	3
Takeda Pharmaceutical Company Limited*	15	9	9			
Shin-Etsu Chemical Co., Ltd.	23	4	4	5	3	3
Mitsubishi Corporation	11	5	5	5	3	3
DENSO Corporation	13	2	2	5	3	2
AVERAGE	12.4	4.0	3.9	4.8	3.1	2.9
		32.4%	31.2%		64.2%	60.0%

* Firms with committee system (not required to have the statutory audit board)
Source: Capital IQ

Tokyo Stock Exchange in terms of the presence of independent directors on those boards.

3.7 Executive Compensation

As discussed earlier, Japanese boards have been functioning like the top management team consisting of mostly insiders or company executives. The promotion to the board or executive level has largely been determined by seniority and internal competition. In terms of executive compensation, the major portion is fixed cash salary, which often rises along with one's seniority with cash bonus which tends to fluctuate by firm performance (Colpan & Yoshikawa, 2012). It is suggested that Japan's executives are undercompensated compared to senior executives in other advanced economies. In order to make Japanese executives pay greater attention to stock performance and provide them with greater financial incentives, institutional investors are pushing for executive compensation with greater proportions of performance-based components, and such a step is being encouraged by the government as well. After the legalization of stock option pay in 1997, stock-based compensation plans have gradually diffused among many Japanese firms and are now in place at most TOPIX 500 companies. However, their compensation design is still rudimentary, their magnitude is rather small as the component of stock and performance-based pay is small, and details of targets, metrics, and calculation formulas are not disclosed (Ethical Boardroom, 2017). Hence, the impact of financial incentives on Japanese executives through their compensation package is still rather weak.

Tables 4 and 5 show the ratio of companies that use stock option pay and performance-based compensation and the CEO compensations of TSE Top 20 firms (with a few firms not disclosing how they compensate their CEOs). As of 2016, 13 out of the Top 20 firms offer stock-based remuneration to their directors.

Table 4 Ratios of Firms that Use Stock Option Pay and Performance-linked Compensation in Japan (2016)

	Stock option (%)	Performance-linked remuneration (%)	Other (%)
Total	31.80	19.80	10.60
JPX-Nikkei 400	45.80	41.80	16.00
TSE First Section	32.10	27.60	13.70
TSE Second Section	15.80	11.90	9.70
Mothers	77.80	7.20	3.10
JASDAQ	30.70	11.10	6.40

Source: Tokyo Stock Exchange

3.8 Ownership Structure

As discussed earlier, ownership structure of listed Japanese firms was characterized by the dominance of stable and strategic domestic shareholders. However, it has gone through significant changes, especially for large firms, and the majority of shares of such firms is owned by institutional investors. Table 6 shows the 10 largest shareholders of Toyota Motor. Among the top shareholders, only Toyota Industries and Denso are affiliated domestic shareholders and the rest appears to be all institutional investors, both foreign and domestic, whereas the company's main banks and affiliated companies were dominant shareholders in the past. This shift from domestic stable ownership to institutional ownership can be seen in many other Japanese firms, suggesting that they are under greater pressure to respond to demands from institutional investors that seek financial returns.

3.9 Conclusions on Corporate Governance in Japan

3.9.1 Summary of Major Trends

Japanese corporate governance has been going through major changes in the past several years, which is reflected in the rising

Table 5 CEO Compensation of the Largest 20 Firms on TSE

		CEO remuneration			
		Base compensation	Bonus	Stock options	Others
1	Toyota Motor Corporation	163,000,000	533,000,000	–	
2	NTT DOCOMO, Inc.	405,000,000	103,000	–	
3	Mitsubishi UFJ Financial Group, Inc.	84,000,000	32,000,000	17,000,000	
4	SoftBank Group Corp.	108,000,000	22,000,000	1,887,000,000	
5	KDDI Corporation	70000000	27000000	–	
6	Nippon Telegraph and Telephone Corporation	558,000,000	93,000,000	–	
7	Japan Post Bank Co., Ltd.	Undisclosed			
8	Honda Motor Co., Ltd.				
9	Sumitomo Mitsui Financial Group, Inc.	91,000,000	22,000,000	10,000,000	
10	Mizuho Financial Group, Inc.	<100,000,000		Introduced in 2008	
11	Keyence Corporation	Undisclosed			
12	Japan Tobacco Inc.	85,000,000	69,000,000	185,000,000	
13	Nissan Motor Co., Ltd.	219,000,000	294,000,000	200,000 shares	15,000,000
14	Fanuc Corporation	Undisclosed			

Table 5 (cont.)

		CEO remuneration			
		Base compensation	**Bonus**	**Stock options**	**Others**
15	Sony Corporation	219,000,000	294,000,000	200,000 shares	15,000,000
16	Canon Inc.	273,000,000	24,000,000	Yes	
17	Takeda Pharmaceutical Company Limited	258,000,000	237,000,000	410,000,000	
18	Shin-Etsu Chemical Co., Ltd.	46850000	21850000	5750000	
19	Mitsubishi Corporation	49933333.33		35888888.89	
20	DENSO Corporation	37000000	23400000		

Source: Capital IQ

Table 6 Largest 10 Shareholders of Toyota Motor Corporation (2016)

Holder	Shareholder type	Shares held	%
Toyota Industries Corporation (TSE:6201)	Corporations (Public)	224515000	7.547
Sumitomo Mitsui Trust Asset Management Co., Ltd.	Traditional Investment Managers	143289675	4.817
Nissay Asset Management Corporation	Traditional Investment Managers	120686000	4.057
DENSO Corporation (TSE:6902)	Corporations (Public)	86882000	2.921
JPMorgan Chase & Co., Private Banking and Investment Banking Investments	Banks/Investment Banks	73483726	2.47
MS&AD Insurance Group Holdings, Inc., Asset Management Arm	Insurance Companies	61711000	2.075
The Vanguard Group, Inc.	Traditional Investment Managers	57021733	1.917
BlackRock, Inc. (NYSE: BLK)	Traditional Investment Managers	51341042	1.726
Nomura Asset Management Co., Ltd.	Traditional Investment Managers	41530900	1.396
Norges Bank Investment Management	Government Pension Sponsors	33006132	1.11

Source: Capital IQ

corporate governance rankings as shown in the introduction. Some initiatives spearheaded by the Abe administration to revitalize Japan's economy and changing ownership structure of many listed Japanese firms were likely major triggers for such changes.

In addition, relatively low levels of corruption in Japan provided a conducive environment for implementation of the major reforms as high levels of corruption often hinder legal and regulatory enforcement in many countries including Asian emerging economies. According to the 2016 Corruption Perceptions Index reported by Transparency International, Japan is the 20th least corrupt nation out of 176 countries, with a score of 72. According to a Forbes article, Japan also has the lowest bribery rate, with only 0.2 percent respondents paying a bribe (Goswami, 2017). This implies that once the new rule is enacted, such rule is usually enforced and most Japanese firms tend to comply with it. The proportion of listed Japanese firms that still do not have independent directors on their board is in the minority today.

Furthermore, pressures from institutional investors on Japanese firms to improve their corporate governance are rising. For example, a proxy advisory firm, International Shareholder Services, is advising against the retired executives to assume advisory positions in the same company, and another advisory firm Glass Lewis is asking higher standards of corporate governance of listed Japanese firms, including greater proportions of independent directors, independent director to chair nomination and remuneration committees (for firms that adopt the committee system), and limitation on multiple directorships of independent directors (Daiwa Research Institute, 2017). The government is also asking institutional investors to disclose their proxy voting practices in details so that those investors would act more responsibly with their votes at the general shareholders' meetings. It is expected that those pressures will impact Japanese corporate governance.

3.9.2   Remaining Challenges

Despite the advance that has been made in the past several years, there are still some remaining challenges. First, the standards required for Japanese firms still lag behind those of other countries. The Corporate Governance Code requires a listed firm to have only two independent directors on its board, whereas the requirements are higher in many other countries – e.g., one-third to over a half on the board. One common comment made by Japanese firms on the difficulty of appointing a greater number of independent directors is that there are not enough individuals who are qualified to be a director. Be that as it may, especially in the transition stage of major institutional change, Japanese firms are perhaps required to exert greater efforts to identify qualified independent directors and also the establishment of some system to train potential directors may be needed.

Another challenge is to move the symbolic and superficial adoption of new practices to more substantive adoption. Most Japanese firms have implemented the required changes in the past few years, including the appointment of independent directors, but there is a risk that many of them are simply engaging in a box-ticking exercise and not fully embracing the spirit of those changes. The recent scandal at Toshiba, even though the company had been known to have an advanced corporate governance system among Japanese firms, indicates this risk. Indeed, in most of Japanese firms, the top executive can heavily influence the appointment of directors including independent directors. If one expects an independent director to play an effective monitoring role, this practice may be problematic. To address those challenges, consistent upgrading of the existing rules and persistent push by key stakeholders such as institutional investors and the government are necessary.

4 Singapore

4.1 Institutional Context

Given its small size, Singapore has heavily been dependent on foreign direct investments for stimulating its economic growth. Foreign direct investments in the manufacturing sector accounted for above 70 percent of gross output, added value, and direct exports until the late 1990s (Tsui-Auch & Yoshikawa, 2010). In other domestic sectors such as finance, which were under government protection, activities of foreign firms were accounted for less, and yet they accounted for over 20 percent of shareholders' equity and equity investments (Tsui-Auch & Yoshikawa, 2015). Hence, in order to attract foreign capital, the Singapore government has been quite keen to maintain strong investor confidence so that foreign firms would continue to invest in the country.

For the economic development and strategic purposes, the state has been a significant owner of commercial assets through government-linked corporations (GLCs) in Singapore. In some sectors, there are some overlaps of political and business leaders. According to Hamilton-Hart (2002), the political leadership is closely interacting with leaders in the private sector and the separation of public and private sectors is quite porous. For instance, in GLCs as well as other firms, we could find former civil servants and ministers having served as board chairs and board members of the United Overseas Bank and the OCBC Bank, two of the three major domestic banks in Singapore, and the other bank is DBS Bank, which is a GLC (Tsui-Auch & Yoshikawa, 2015).

Corporate governance system in Singapore is largely modeled after the Anglo-American model, especially the UK model, which relies on capital market discipline of managerial decision-making (Prowse, 1998). However, because the capital market in Singapore is thin compared to that in the United States and the United Kingdom with only over 700 listed companies on the Singapore Exchange, and equity is held among a small group of block shareholders including the Singapore Government, family owners, multinational and regional corporations, and wealthy individuals, takeovers are extremely rare (Phan & Yoshikawa, 2004). This implies that capital market discipline on managerial behavior in Singapore is not as strict as that in the United States and the United Kingdom.

4.2 Ownership and Control in Domestic Firms

As the majority of companies (including government-linked and family-controlled enterprises) have a block shareholder that holds an equity interest of 15 percent or more (Tan, Tan & Ching, 2006), a clear separation between ownership and management is often lacking in many listed companies in Singapore. Given the weak market discipline through hostile takeovers and weak minority shareholder activism, it is suggested that the state has been the principal player or guardian in terms of corporate governance for listed firms (Gourevitch & Shinn, 2005), even though institutional investors hold large equity stakes in large listed firms as shown in Table 7.

4.3 The Impact of the Asian Financial Crisis

The Asian Financial Crisis in 1997, which was triggered by the sharp drop in the value of the Thai baht, significantly damaged the confidence of foreign investors and subsequently led to drastic economic decline. Compared to other economies in the region, however, the impact on the Singapore economy was relatively modest, and yet domestic banks in Singapore were affected by the sharp decline in property prices as well as the political and economic changes in South-East Asian countries, as those banks were exposed to those economies through their business networks. After the crisis, IMF economists as well as external consultants (Economist Intelligence Unit and Andersen Consulting, 2000) advised Asian business and political leaders to professionalize their corporate management and improve their corporate governance structures. Even though Singapore did not receive any financial assistance from IMF, such advice sent an important message about how external professionals including investors look at the business practices in the region.

The crisis gave a strong impetus for the Singapore government to restructure its economy for it to become more competitive in the global capital markets so that foreign investors would continue to invest in the country. The government aimed to build Singapore as not just a regional or Asian financial hub, but rather a global financial hub where foreign capital is attracted from around the world. For that objective, global institutional investors must feel

Table 7 Shareholding by State Investment Arms and Institutional Shareholders in the Largest 20 Firms in Singapore

Rank	Company	Board size	No. of ID	CEO-chair duality	No. of government-linked directors
1	Singapore Telecommunications Limited	11	6	No	2
2	DBS Group Holdings Limited	9	6	No	2
3	Singapore Exchange Limited	12	7	No	4
4	CapitaLand Limited	10	9	No	4
5	Singapore Press Holdings Limited	11	10	No	3 (1 formally linked)
6	SATS Limited	10	9	No	2 (1 formally linked)
7	Keppel Land Limited	9	6	No	0
8	Singapore Post Limited*	12	6	No	0
9	SMRT Corporation Limited	10	9	No	0
10	Keppel Telecommunications and Transportation Limited	8	5	No	0
11	Singapore Airlines Limited	9	8	No	1
12	StarHub Limited	11	5	No	0
13	Singapore Technologies Engineering Limited	15	10	No	1
14	Keppel Corporation Limited	10	7	No	1 formally linked
15	Sembcorp Industries Limited	11	8	No	5
16	Global Logistic Properties Limited	10	8	No	3 (2 formally linked)
17	Yoma Strategic Holdings Limited	8	4	No	0
18	Oversea-Chinese Banking Corporation Limited	10	7	No	3
19	City Developments Limited	8	6	Yes	0
20	Fraser and Neave Limited	9	3	No	0

Source: Company annual reports

that Singapore has high standards in terms of regulatory oversights including corporate governance practices of local firms. For such investors especially from advanced economies where corporate governance standards are high, good corporate governance is one key mechanism that functions to monitor managerial decision-making and improves transparency, which allows those investors to make informed investment decisions.

4.4 Corporate Governance Codes of 2001 and 2005

The government started to reform a corporate governance system in Singapore in the late 1990s, which subsequently led to the issuance of the Code of Corporate Governance 2001. The Ministry of Finance and the Monetary Authority of Singapore (MAS) set up the Corporate Governance Committee in 1999 for the objective of making recommendations on a code of corporate governance after it investigated best governance practices globally. The Committee introduced a code of corporate governance in 2001 and implemented it from 2003. The Singapore Exchange adopted this rule and required all listed companies to comply or explain if there were any discrepancies (Tsui-Auch & Yoshikawa, 2015). The code touched on four areas; board matters, remuneration, accountability and audit, and communications with shareholders.

While the principles of the code are similar to those in Anglo-American countries such as the United States and Australia, there were some differences due to some unique local conditions in Singapore (Tsui-Auch & Yoshikawa, 2015). One such difference was that the Singaporean code requires a minimum of one-third of board members to be independent, while the codes or rules in the United Kingdom, the United States, and Australia require at least 50 percent. Another difference was that a director was regarded as independent in the Singaporean code if he or she does not receive aggregate payments not related to directors' fees exceeding SGD 200,000 from the firm for which he or she serves as a director. However, codes in many other countries do not allow any payment from the firm in order to for an outside director to be treated as independent. These changes likely reflected the government's effort to implement high corporate governance standards and yet made them more acceptable to the local companies.

The revised code was issued in 2005 and implemented in 2007 after the Council on Corporate Disclosure and Governance established in 2002 reviewed the existing code. The existing code was not significantly revised, but there was one change on the requirements on the Nominating Committee (NC). In the 2001 code, NC needs to have at least three directors of which two of them including the chairperson should be independent. In the 2005 code, the chairperson of NC needs to be an independent director with no direct association with a substantial shareholder that holds at least 5 percent voting shares. Since many Singaporean companies have block owners, this inclusion is an attempt to mitigate the influence of such owners on the selection of senior executives and directors.

4.5   Corporate Governance Code of 2012

MAS issued a revised Code of Corporate Governance on May 2, 2012. The revised code includes several changes in some key areas such as director independence, multiple directorship, and information disclosure.

4.5.1   Director Independence

One of the major changes in the revised code is that it now requires a greater proportion (more than 50 percent from 33 percent in the previous code) of independent directors on the board where: (a) the Chairman of the Board (the "Chairman") and the chief executive officer (or equivalent) (the "CEO") is the same person; (b) the Chairman and the CEO are immediate family members; (c) the Chairman is part of the management team; or (d) the Chairman is not an independent director. The code also stipulates that every company should appoint an independent director to be the lead independent director.

The code also touches on the relationship between the board chair and chief executive officer. It is stated in the code that "there should be a clear division of responsibilities between the leadership of the Board and the executives responsible for managing the company's business. No one individual should represent a considerable concentration of power. The relationship between the Chairman and the CEO should be disclosed, if they are immediate family members." Also, as recommended in other countries, the code also stipulates that "independent directors should meet periodically without the presence of the other directors, and the lead independent director should provide feedback to the Chairman after such meetings." These are an attempt to make the separation of the execution and monitoring function much clearer.

These changes have made the requirement on the proportion of independent directors at the same level as in many other countries. The revised code also has additional instances where a director will be deemed non-independent. These changes attempt to tighten the definition of independence and thereby improving the effectiveness of board monitoring function. Specifically, it says that:

- If he, or his immediate family members, in the current or immediate past financial year, is or was a 10 percent shareholder of, a partner in (with a 10 percent or more stake), an executive officer of, or a director of, any organization to/from which the company or its subsidiaries made/received significant payments or material services (which may include auditing, banking, consulting, and legal services) in the current or immediate past financial year.
- The independence of any director who has served on the Board **beyond nine years** from the date of his first appointment should be subject to particularly rigorous review.
- A director will be deemed non-independent if the director or an immediate family member of the director accepts any significant

compensation from the company or any of its related corporations for the provision of services for the current or immediate past financial year, other than compensation for Board service. A company's "related corporations" include its holding company and fellow subsidiaries, in addition to its "subsidiaries."

Tables 8 and 9 show the changes in the board structure, the number of lead directors, and the recent board composition of large listed companies in Singapore.

4.5.2 Multiple Directorships

Another change was about multiple board memberships. Many outside directors in Singapore have multiple directorships. However, there is a growing debate on the negative effects of "busy" directors not only in Singapore but also in other counties. It is suggested that a director with too many directorships cannot play an effective managerial monitoring role (Fich & Shivdasani, 2006). This revision is hence a response to such concern. The followings are specific changes:

• When evaluating the director's suitability, the Nominating Committee (NC) should take into consideration the director's number of listed company Board representations, and other principal commitments.

• The Board should determine the maximum number of listed company Board representations any director may hold, and disclose this in the annual report.

4.5.3 Executive Remuneration

The revised code has enhanced the information disclosure of executive remuneration. One such requirement is that remuneration for each individual director, and the CEO on a named basis to the nearest thousand dollars. Disclosure of director and CEO remuneration was only made based on some bands prior to the revised code of 2012. This change has moved the level of remuneration disclosure in Singapore closer to some other countries when listed companies disclose quite detailed remuneration information. In addition to remuneration to directors and the CEO, total

Table 8 Board Structure Changes of Listed Firms in Singapore

	2013	2014	2015	2016
Independent chair	14.8%	16.9%	18.4%	19.9%
Non-independent and non-executive chair	15.4%	13.2%	18.2%	Na
Having lead independent director	35.2%	43.9%	53.8%	68.0%

Description		**2014**		**2016**	
IDs forming at least half the board (all firms)	Large-cap firms	55%	62%	62%	65%
	Mid-cap firms		46%		61%
Number of Lead IDs		304		396	
Board size		6		6.6	

Sources: ISCA (2014, 2016); Cai Hao Xiang, *Business Times* (2016)

Table 9 Board Structure of the 20 Largest Listed Companies in Singapore*

	Company	State ownership	Institutional ownership (except for state)
1	Singapore Telecommunications Limited	51 (TH)	45.33
2	DBS Group Holdings Limited	11.18 (TH)	88.68
3	Singapore Exchange Limited	0	75.66
4	CapitaLand Limited	39.57 (TH)	47.25
5	Singapore Press Holdings Limited	0	40.92
6	SATS Limited	43.34 (TH)	41.85
7	Keppel Land Limited	20.91 (TH)	9.91
8	Singapore Post Limited	36.64 (TH), deemed interest through DBS & STL	49.84
9	SMRT Corporation Limited	54.1 (TH)	17.94
10	Keppel Telecommunications and Transportation Limited	79.37 (TH) deemed interest through Keppel Corporation	10.28
11	Singapore Airlines Limited	55.33 (TH)	30.04
12	StarHub Limited	56.54 (TH)	20.68
13	Singapore Technologies Engineering Limited	49.99 (TH)	37.28
14	Keppel Corporation Limited	20.49	50.64
15	Sembcorp Industries Limited	48.82 (TH)	36
16	Global Logistic Properties Limited	37 (GIC)	94.7

Table 9 (cont.)

	Company	State ownership	Institutional ownership (except for state)
17	Yoma Strategic Holdings Limited	0	82.79
18	Oversea-Chinese Banking Corporation Limited	0	45.04
19	City Developments Limited	0	63.09
20	Fraser and Neave Limited	0	93.71

Source: Company annual reports
* By market capitalization based on the ASEAN Corporate Governance Scorecard (ACGS)

aggregate remuneration paid to the top five key management personnel, who are not also directors or the CEO, should be disclosed under the revised code. Furthermore, disclosure of remuneration of employees who are immediate family members of a director or the CEO, and whose remuneration exceeds SGD 50,000, instead of SGD 150,000 as in the 2005 code, is required in the revised code. Finally, the company has to disclose information on the link between performance and remuneration paid to the executive directors and key management personnel. Compared to the code of 2001, the revised code of 2012 is a significant improvement in terms of the disclosure of executive remuneration.

4.5.4 Other Changes

One of other changes is about a company's risk management. The board's review of the company's internal control systems (should be conducted at least annually) should include financial, operational, compliance, and information technology controls and risk managements systems. The requirements on information technology and risk management systems reflect changing technology environments that companies face in recent years. Another key change is related to the composition of audit committee (AC). The 2005 code only requires at least two AC members to have recent and relevant accounting or related financial management expertise. It does not specifically require the AC chairperson to have such expertise. In the 2012 code, however, the AC chairperson and at least one more AC member should have recent and relevant accounting or related financial management expertise or experience.

4.6   Corporate Governance Practices

The past corporate governance codes (2001, 2005, 2012) continuously raised the corporate governance standards and requirements in Singapore. Perhaps due to these improvements, Singapore consistently ranked as one of the top countries in Asia in terms of the quality of corporate governance as shown in the introduction. For example, the use of long-term incentives (LTIs) for executive compensation has been increasing especially among large companies in Singapore. Twenty-five percent of the surveyed companies awarded their executives with LTIs, 16 percent implementing stock option pay, and 14 percent awarding shares in 2012 (Hay Group, 2013). If we look at the utilization of such plans by company size, less than 50 percent of large firms, about 33 percent of medium-sized firms, and less than 25 percent of small firms used LTIs for their executives in 2012. The ratio of companies that used LTIs increased to 28 percent in 2013. The increase was particularly noticeable among large firms where 86 percent of the surveyed companies used LTIs in 2013, while 32 percent of medium-sized firms and 17 percent of small firms did in 2013 (Hay Group, 2014). This trend indicates that boards in Singaporean firms are paying greater attention to linking executives' financial incentives to the firm's long-term performance.

Table 10 CEO Remuneration Change from 2012 to 2015 in
Singapore

CEO pay (in thousand SGD per annum)	2012	2013	2014	2015
Large-cap	3878	4743	4073	3875
Medium-cap	1625	2000	1863	1625
Small-cap	750	625	643	713
All	1125	1092	1125	1101

Source: Equide (2015)

In addition, CEO compensation in listed firms in Singapore has
not gone up much since 2012 as shown in Table 10. This trend
suggests that boards of listed Singaporean firms are rather prudent
in setting the levels of CEO compensation, presumably by linking it
to firm performance.

4.7 Government's Role in Corporate Governance in Singapore

One of the characteristics of corporate governance in Singapore is a
heavy involvement of the government's investment arms in its
portfolio companies. In other countries where the state is heavily
involved in the domestic business, board representations and
equity ownership are common methods to exert its influence on
management and key decision-makings. As of 2016, 29 percent of
Temasek Holdings' portfolio was directed toward investments in
Singapore (Temasak 2016 Review). Looking at the table presented
earlier, several companies in the largest 20 firms have directors
who are linked to the government (Temasek or GIC).

Temasek has a direct shareholding (above 5 percent) in 7 of the
largest 50 companies listed on the SGX, and owns more than
50 percent of the shares in three of them. If we also consider
indirect interests, Temasek has a greater than 5 percent stake in
17 companies, including 9 of which it has a greater than 50 percent

stakes. Furthermore, we also identified 42 other listed and unlisted companies in Singapore associated with Temasek (Chen, 2016). The table shown earlier indicates that state ownership through its investment arms remains one key feature of corporate governance in Singapore.

One unique aspect of the state ownership in Singapore is that listed government-linked companies or GLCs usually have high corporate governance standards than other listed companies. GLCs tend to have larger proportions of independent directors and have greater information disclosure especially compared to family-controlled firms (Tsui-Auch & Yoshikawa, 2015). A survey of the directors of the top 50 listed companies on the SGX showed no strong evidence of Temasek directly appointing nominee directors to a company board (Chen, 2016). Indeed, GLCs have been perceived as a role-model in terms of corporate governance that other firms should emulate (Tsui-Auch & Yoshikawa, 2010). This is an important difference from state-owned firms in other countries particularly in developing economies.

4.8   Conclusions on Corporate Governance in Singapore

4.8.1   Summary of Major Trends

The Singapore government has been steadily raising standards of corporate governance since it first issued the corporate governance code in 2001. The requirements in the recent code are almost comparable to those in the codes in other advanced economies. As evidence of its high corporate governance standards, Singapore often ranks as the top corporate governance country in Asia (CG Watch, 2016). Despite it has been ranked as the best in Asia, the Singapore government is planning to review the code for further improvement. In February 2017, the MAS formed a Corporate Governance Council to review the application of the revised 2012 Code of Corporate Governance. Representatives from the MAS, the Accounting and Corporate Regulatory Authority (ACRA) and the SGX are on this Council (MAS, 2017). It seems that the government is well aware of the need to review the existing rules to stay in the top position because other countries may catch up by adopting higher requirements. As good reputation in its corporate governance system is critical to be a global financial hub, Singapore presumably has strong incentives to keep improving its governance standards.

4.8.2　Remaining Challenges

One of the potential challenges that Singapore may face is the relatively weak pressure from shareholders due to high owner-ship concentration of listed companies and the lack of share-holder activism. Because of this ownership structure of many Singaporean firms, the government needs to continue to play an active role in improving corporate governance standards. Further, as many listed companies in Singapore are relatively small and often family-owned, higher corporate governance requirements entails cost that those companies may find too onerous. As in other Asian economies, improving corporate governance of smaller family-owned companies requires greater efforts than that of large companies.

5　Korea

5.1　Institutional Context

Business group–affiliated (chaebol) companies such as Samsung Group and LG Corporation dominated Korean business and domes-tic economy in the pre-financial crisis period before 1997. Founding family owners controlled their group companies with limited own-ership stakes through pyramid and cross shareholding structure, which allowed them to exert control without a majority stake. There was no mandatory requirement to have independent directors on Korean boards to monitor management, and hence there was no effective managerial oversight. Furthermore, as those business groups received preferential treatment from the Korean government, management of those groups were well protected from external stakeholders as well as from competition in the domestic market.

Similar to other Asian economies, the Asian Financial Crisis in 1997 forced the government and the Korean business groups to make drastic changes including their corporate governance practices. The crisis imposed devastating damages to the Korean economy as the country faced with the risk of default when foreign capital flowed out of the country and many companies including large chaebol group firms went bankrupt. Poor corporate governance was often cited by observers and analysts as one of the reasons for the economic crisis in Korea (Tsui-Auch, Yang, & Yoshikawa, 2016). Facing the dire economic condition, President Kim needed to seek financial assistance from the IMF and the World Bank.

As conditions for their financial support, those international organizations requested the Korean government to implement various radical reform measures including corporate governance reforms (Ahmadjian & Son, 2004). The government liberalized the domestic market to foreign investors for direct and portfolio investments, and the limit on foreign ownership of listed firms was eventually removed. These changes started to expose the domestic firms to pressures from those foreign investors. This was a drastic change for many Korean firms that had not experienced such pressure in the pre-crisis period. Due to the reform measures, much improved corporate governance mechanisms such as more independent boards and greater information disclosure were adopted.

One of the major corporate governance measures implemented after the crisis was a requirement of independent directors on boards of listed companies. The legal change in 2000 requires a listed company with assets of over KRW 2 trillion to have at least a half of its board to be occupied by independent directors. Following this new legal requirement, the number of independent directors on Korean boards had increased. However, many firms often resisted the implementation of the reform measures, for example, by reducing the board size so that they could minimize the number of independent directors to be appointed on their boards. One survey shows that over 70 percent of chaebol-affiliated firms had only one or two outside directors from 2001 to 2003, soon after the new requirement was implemented (OECD, 2004).

Furthermore, chaebol-affiliated firms often appointed executives of other group firms on their boards although their independence was questionable. In addition, former and current politicians as well as public officials were often appointed as independent directors in order to establish linkages with the government (Choi, Park, & Yoo, 2007). One study also shows that firms had greater proportions of outsiders on their boards when the state has greater control, prior performance is poor, foreign ownership is high, and debt levels are high (Chizema & Kim, 2010), indicating that firms show greater compliance when they needed to do so to appease external stakeholders such as the government and foreign investors. These practices suggest that despite the stringent requirement on board independence, business group owners and executives could still stifle managerial monitoring by board.

5.2   Recent Developments

In view of the frequent corporate scandals in Korea, a renewed focus on Korea's corporate governance is publicly debated, and organizations such as Korea Corporate Governance Service (KCGS) are trying to improve it especially regarding the complex chaebol issues in Korea. KCGS is an organization that provides environment, social, and governance (ESG) ratings; proxy voting; and socially responsible investment (SRI) consulting, among other services (Oh & Ahn, 2015).

In 2012 presidential election, despite tough law enforcements, regulatory reforms against the chaebols have been rather limited due to strong opposition of those groups. Nonetheless, the following reforms have still been made in the last few years:
a) Mandatory disclosure of remuneration
   Amendments to the Financial Investment Services and Capital Markets Act (Capital Markets Acts) in May 2013 has enforced the requirement for listed companies to disclose the remuneration of individual directors and executive officers who receive an amount equal to or higher than KRW 500 million.

Also in 2013, to encourage board of directors to be more responsible with regard to risk management, a plan has been formulated by the Financial Services Commission (FSC) to require board of directors to establish and disclose a remuneration system in accordance with their accomplishments and responsibilities.

b) Cessation of shadow voting system from 2015 onwards
Through shadow voting system, companies were able to meet quorum requirement to pass resolutions with the help of the Korea Securities Depository, which cast votes on behalf of absent shareholders in proportion to actual votes. This system was only allowed until 2015, and will be replaced by electronic voting as well as proxy solicitation.

c) Corporate Governance Code for financial institutions
In November 2014, FSC released the Corporate Governance Code for financial institutions requiring them to publish a more detailed corporate governance annual report and explain their current governance under a comply-or-explain principle to promote the monitoring activities within the market, planning to assess the corporate governance annual report through the assessment-specialized institution.

d) Korean Stewardship Code
Korean Stewardship Council chaired by Professor Myoeng Hyeong Cho of Korea University Business School issued Korea's first stewardship code in December 2016. The code aims to propose key principles for institutional investors to exercise their stewardship responsibilities effectively.

5.3 Board Structure

As discussed, Korea responded to the Asian Financial Crisis by passing a law under the Korean Commercial Code that requires a majority of board members of large listed companies (assets exceeding KRW 2 trillion) to comprise of independent directors. For smaller companies, the requirement is only a quarter of board members to be independent directors. Since then, the laws have remained largely unchanged, although the commercial code has constantly refined the requirements for companies to establish independence of independent directors.

Looking at the professional backgrounds of independent directors in Korean firms, there has been a continual decrease in independent directors with background in business and management among KOSPI (Korea Composite Stock Price Index) market listed firms from 45.2 percent in 2004 to 28.4 percent in 2011. According to public disclosure of 93 listed companies belonging to Korea's 10 largest chaebols or business groups, 68 independent directors were appointed in 2013, and among them 28 individuals (41.2 percent) were former government officials, including 10 from the National Tax Service. This trend presents an interest comparison to independent directors in firms in some other countries; for example, the United States where many independent directors are former or current CEOs or senior executives of other firms. Nevertheless, the proportions of independent directors in listed Korean firms have been increasing as shown in Table 11, and many large

Table 11 Board Size and the Number of Independent Director in Large Korean Firms

	Board size	**No. of ID**
Samsung Electronics	12	5
Hyundai Motor	9	5
SK Hynix	10	7
Korea Electric Power	15	8
Naver Corporation	7	4
Hyundai Mobis	7	4
Samsung Life Insurance	8	2
POSCO	12	6
Shinhan Financial Group	12	10
Amorepacific Group	7	4

Sources: Company annual reports

firms now have over a half of their board seats occupied by independent directors.

5.4 Executive Compensation

Korea has been slow in improving the public disclosure of executive compensation. It was only in 2014 with the amendment of the Financial Investment Services and Capital Markets Act (FISCMA) that the compensation of individual executives earning above KRW 500 million needs to be disclosed. Prior to 2014, only the aggregated compensation of all executives was needed to be disclosed. In addition, there was no requirement for companies to disclose the components of executive compensation and only the aggregated amount is required to be reported. As such, it was difficult to assess the portion of performance-related components Korean firms used in their executive pay structure. While the current disclosure standards might deter excessively high pay for executive, it may be an insufficient deterrence as highly paid family directors in chaebol firms may not be registered as firm executives (Kim, Lee, & Chin, 2017). It is also difficult to assess whether the executive pay package is appropriate as companies do not have to disclose detailed structure of their compensation. Even after the introduction of the disclosure standards, executive pay continued to rise; hence its deterrence effect appears to be limited (Kim et al., 2017). As for the level of executive compensation, Korean executives in large firms such as Samsung Electronics received comparable pay as executives at major US firms based on the disclosed information as Table 12 shows.

5.5 Ownership Structure

Since the liberalization of capital markets after the Asian Financial Crisis, shareholdings by institutional investors in Korean firms have increased significantly and they now hold large stakes in many large firms. As Table 13 shows, public pension funds and professional investment firms own large equity stakes in Samsung

Table 12 Highest Paid Executives of Samsung Electronics

Samsung Electronics	Salary	Bonus	Other
Kwon, Oh-Hyun	20,830	4837	8034
Shin, Jong-Kyun	17,280	3054	170
Yoon, Boo-Keun	17,280	1921	480

Figures are in million KRW: USD 1 is approx. KRW 1150 (from December 2016 to May 2017)
Source: Company annual reports

Table 13 Largest 20 Shareholders in Samsung Electronics and Hyundai Motor (2016)

Samsung Electronics Co., Ltd.			
Holder	Owner type	Common stock equivalently held	% of CSO
National Pension Service	Government Pension Sponsors	12,976,838	9.4
Samsung Life Insurance Co., Ltd. (KOSE: A032830)	Corporations (public)	11,152,107	8.1
Samsung C&T Corporation (KOSE: A028260)	Corporations (public)	5,976,362	4.3
Lee, Kun-Hee (Former Chairman of the Board)	Individuals/Insiders	4,997,862	3.6
Capital Research and Management Company	Traditional Investment Managers	4,305,402	3.1
BlackRock, Inc. (NYSE: BLK)	Traditional Investment Managers	3,284,035	2.4
Union Asset Management Holding AG	Traditional Investment Managers	3,230,550	2.4
The Vanguard Group, Inc.	Traditional Investment Managers	2,538,618	1.8

Table 13 (cont.)

Samsung Electronics Co., Ltd.			
Holder	Owner type	Common stock equivalently held	% of CSO
Samsung Fire & Marine Insurance Co., Ltd. (KOSE:A000810)	Corporations (Public)	1,856,370	1.4
Franklin Resources, Inc. (NYSE:BEN)	Traditional Investment Managers	1,846,272	1.3
Dodge & Cox	Traditional Investment Managers	1,538,239	1.1
Norges Bank Investment Management	Government Pension Sponsors	1,375,500	1.0
Aberdeen Asset Management PLC (LSE:ADN)	Traditional Investment Managers	1,175,980	0.9
Hong, Ra Hui	Individuals/Insiders	1,083,072	0.8
Samsung Asset Management Co. Ltd.	Traditional Investment Managers	1,010,680	0.7
FMR LLC	Traditional Investment Managers	857,517	0.6
Lee, Jae-Yong (Vice Chairman)	Individuals/Insiders	840,403	0.6
Genesis Asset Managers, LLP	Traditional Investment Managers	790,826	0.6
T. Rowe Price Group, Inc. (NasdaqGS: TROW)	Traditional Investment Managers	741,767	0.5
Artisan Partners Limited Partnership	Traditional Investment Managers	683,879	0.5
J.P. Morgan Asset Management, Inc.	Traditional Investment Managers	646,994	0.5
Mirae Asset Global Investments Co., Ltd	Traditional Investment Managers	624,333	0.5

Table 13 (cont.)

Hyundai Motor Company			
Holder	Owner Type	Common Stock Equivalent Held	% of CSO
Hyundai Mobis Co., Ltd. (KOSE: A012330)	Corporations (Public)	45,782,023	22.1
National Pension Service	Government Pension Sponsors	17,890,250	8.6
Capital Research and Management Company	Traditional Investment Managers	12,054,853	5.8
Mong-Koo, Jung (Chairman and Chief Executive Officer)	Individuals/Insiders	11,395,859	5.5
Franklin Resources, Inc. (NYSE:BEN)	Traditional Investment Managers	5,938,648	2.9
Chung, Eui-sun (Vice Chairman)	Individuals/Insiders	5,017,145	2.4
BlackRock, Inc. (NYSE:BLK)	Traditional Investment Managers	4,625,189	2.2
The Vanguard Group, Inc.	Traditional Investment Managers	3,089,046	1.5
Dimensional Fund Advisors LP	Traditional Investment Managers	2,635,004	1.3
Norges Bank Investment Management	Government Pension Sponsors	1,958,008	0.9
Tweedy, Browne Company LLC	Traditional Investment Managers	1,695,985	0.8
Samsung Asset Management Co. Ltd.	Traditional Investment Managers	1,376,279	0.7

Table 13 (cont.)

Hyundai Motor Company			
Holder	Owner Type	Common Stock Equivalent Held	% of CSO
Mackenzie Financial Corporation	Traditional Investment Managers	1,121,854	0.5
Eastspring Investments (Singapore) Limited	Traditional Investment Managers	1,108,253	0.5
Capfi Delen Asset Management NV	Traditional Investment Managers	890,750	0.4
Korea Investment Management Co., Ltd.	Traditional Investment Managers	884,743	0.4
J.P. Morgan Asset Management, Inc.	Traditional Investment Managers	867,867	0.4
T. Rowe Price Group, Inc. (NasdaqGS: TROW)	Traditional Investment Managers	832,132	0.4
Mirae Asset Global Investments Co., Ltd.	Traditional Investment Managers	803,114	0.4
International Value Advisers, LLC	Traditional Investment Managers	783,162	0.4
Teachers Insurance and Annuity Association of America – College Retirement Equities Fund	Traditional Investment Managers	602,783	0.3

Source: www.4-traders.com/KOSPI-COMPOSITE-INDEX-2355012/
components/

Electronics and Hyundai Motor, the two largest firms in Korea. At the same time, it is also noticeable that other group-affiliated firms still hold large stakes, and the founding family members appear on the large shareholder list although their shareholdings are not significant.

5.6 Conclusions on Corporate Governance in Korea

5.6.1 Summary of Major Trends

The initial trigger for major changes in Korean corporate governance was the Asian Finance Crisis. Soon after the crisis, the Korean government implemented a series of reform measures. Consequently, there have been major changes in corporate governance practices among Korean firms. The presence of institutional and foreign investment management firms have been increasing as major shareholders. There have also been significant improvements in the formal structure such as the proportions of independent directors on Korean boards. Listed companies are now required to disclose the remuneration of individual directors and executive officers who receive an amount equal to or higher than KRW 500 million. They also publish a more detailed corporate governance annual report and explain current governance under a comply-or-explain principle. The board has increased responsibility for risk management. Finally, the issuance of the Stewardship Code in 2016 pushed institutional investors to be responsible for managing their assets of their clients prudently by monitoring their investee firms.

5.6.2 Remaining Challenges

Despite all these reforms and changes, corporate governance in Korea is still ranked relatively low; ranked eighth out of 11 Asian economies in 2016 in the CG Watch report (CLSA and ACGA, 2016). One possible reason is Korean's political culture. For example, according to the 2016 Corruption Perceptions Index reported by Transparency International, Korea is the 52nd least corrupt nation out of 176 countries. Korea's 2016 corruption rank dropped 15 placing from 37th least corrupt country out of 175 countries in 2015. In the OECD corruption rankings, South Korea now ranks 29th out of 35 countries, which is a much lower score than that in 2015 (26th). This came after the international committee has evaluated the results of Korea and concluded that corruption rate has increased in Korea's public sector. Even before the presidential scandal in 2016, there were a couple of other structural corruption cases involving bribery among those who held political power.

The newly implemented Kim Young-ran Act in 2016 aims to make a fundamental change in Korea. This act is supposed to suppress the use of gift-giving to gain favor from individuals working in public office, the media, and educational institutions. Such practice was widespread in Korea that experienced the drastic drop in corruption rankings after the uncovering of the political scandal involving Choi Soon-sil (wife of Chung Yoon-hoi, former chief of staff to President Park Geun-hye).

Nonetheless, the revelation of the Choi Soon-sil scandal has proved to show that national laws and policies have failed to address this problem, and they have come "a means of securing the private interests of presidential aides, and the chaebols' self-interests have been revived" (Transparency Korea Chapter, 2017). These events have jeopardized the Korean economy and the reputation of its business practices, and Transparency International-Korea has strongly recommended a set of anti-corruption policies to rebuild national anti-corruption laws and promote transparency and, subsequently, to rebuild public trust. Such political environment can inevitably weaken the government's enforcement effectiveness, including the rules on corporate governance.

Related to this issue is the resistance by some chaebol leaders to reform their corporate governance substantively. Former President Park Geun-hye called for democratization of the Korean economy by regulating chaebols and enforcing fair market competition by strict legal enforcement so that the economic gaps between haves and have-nots can be lessened. However, regulatory reforms have been limited due to strong opposition by chaebols (Oh & Ahn, 2015). The impeachment of President Park and the bribery scandal involving the heir of the Samsung Group may lead to more effective regulations of chaebols. However, it is premature to predict how the situation will progress with the new president has just been elected.

6 China

6.1 Institutional Context

Stock exchanges in China have a short history with the first stock exchange being opened in Shanghai in December 1990 and then in Shenzhen in July 1991. Under the communist rule, it was a new and important step for Chinese companies to be able to allow their stock shares to be publicly traded. The China Securities Regulatory Commission (CSRS) founded in 1992 is a securities regulatory body responsible for approving initial public offerings (IPOs) and regulating securities companies among other things. Through CSRS the government controlled the IPO, and even though securities companies and investment banks began to play an important role in the IPO over time, CSRC still controls the IPO process as the entity that has the final approval authority (Jiang & Kim, 2015).

Because of the short history of stock exchanges in China, ownership structure of listed companies has changed in a rather unique fashion. Chinese shares are divided into tradable and non-tradable shares, and controlling owners owned non-tradable shares while tradable shares were mostly owned by individual investors, who were generally short-term speculators, in early years. Overtime, however, shareholdings by institutional investors have increased, especially in recent years, while state owners maintained high equity ownership. All non-tradable shares began to become tradable shares in 2005, and state ownership was gradually converted to tradable shares, which pushed up state ownership in tradable shares. In 2012, institutional investors including mutual funds owned about 17 percent, individuals about 25 percent, and state owners owned about 57 percent of tradable shares in 2012 (Jiang & Kim, 2015), suggesting that state owners are a significant player in listed Chinese companies.

6.2   Code of Corporate Governance for Listed Companies 2002

In the wake of the Asian Financial Crisis, regulatory bodies in many countries including Singapore and Korea started to introduce corporate governance codes for the first time. China similarly followed the trend and issued its own corporate governance code in 2002, which provides very general guidelines on how companies should be governed. In the code, the chapter that outlines rules for directors and boards of directors contains the followings:

- The number of directors and the structure of the board of directors shall be in compliance with laws and regulations and shall ensure the effective discussion and efficient, timely, and prudent decision-making process of the board of directors. A listed company shall formulate rules of procedure for its board of directors in its articles of association to ensure the board of directors' efficient function and rational decisions.
- A listed company shall introduce independent directors to its board of directors in accordance with relevant regulations. Independent directors shall be independent from the listed company that employs them and the company's major shareholders. In a listed company an independent director may not hold any other position apart from independent director.
- A listed company shall formulate rules of procedure for its board of directors in its articles of association to ensure the board of directors' efficient function and rational decisions.
- The board of directors of a listed company may establish a corporate strategy committee, an audit committee, a nomination committee, a remuneration and appraisal committee, and other

special committees in accordance with the resolutions of the shareholders' meetings. All committees shall be composed solely of directors. The audit committee, the nomination committee, and the remuneration and appraisal committee shall be chaired by an independent director, and independent directors shall constitute the majority of the committees. At least one independent director from the audit committee shall be an accounting professional.

Generally, these rules are not specific and contain prescriptions that are expected to be followed regardless of the presence of the code. However, the last point on committees stipulates a potentially important issue, i.e., the audit, nomination, and remuneration committees to be chaired by independent directors and the majority of members of each committee should be independent directors. Despite the short history of China's stock exchanges, this clause is progressive as it is only recent that other jurisdictions have started to require independent committee chairs.

The code also has a rule on managerial compensation as follows. Again, the rule is quite general and does not offer any specific guideline as to how each firm should design its compensation package.

- A listed company shall establish rewarding systems that link the compensation for management personnel to the company's performance and to the individual's work performance. The results of the performance assessment shall be approved by the board of directors, explained at the shareholders' meetings, and disclosed.

There are different formal requirements on the establishment of board system and board structure by the Chinese Corporate Law (CCL) and CSRC. CCL requires a listed firm to have a board with the required board size to be from 5 to 19. CSRC's requirement on a listed firm was to have at least two independent directors by June 30, 2002, and one-third of outside directors on a board by June 30, 2003. Currently, Chinese listed firms are still required to have one-third of the members to be independent. Non-listed firms and wholly state-owned enterprises are not required to have a board.

Table 14 Percentage of Firms with State Ownership in China

Year	2012	2013	2014	2015	2016
State	20.02%	18.37%	19.23%	19.25%	20.61%
Non-state	79.98%	81.62%	80.77%	81.00%	79.39%

Source: CSMAR

6.3   SASAC of the State Council

State-owned Assets Supervision and Administration Commission of the State Council (SASAC) is a special commission of the People's Republic of China, directly under the State Council. SASAC currently oversees 102 centrally owned companies (SASAC, 2017). Companies directly supervised by SASAC are continuously reduced through mergers, according to the state-owned enterprise restructuring plan, with the number of SASAC companies down from over 150 in 2008 (Chiang, 2008). However, China's state-owned economy remains significant today (*The Economist*, September 19, 2015). State-owned firms' exact contributions to the country's industrial output is debated, but has been estimated at between 25 percent and 30 percent. State-owned firms continue to enjoy advantages in obtaining bank loans and regulatory approvals, even if their privileged capital access has gradually declined (Leutert, 2016). Table 14 shows that the percentage of companies with the state ownership has not changed much from 2012 to 2016.

6.4   Legal and Regulatory Changes Related to Corporate Governance

One of the major regulatory changes related to corporate governance is the split share reform in 2005. The reform is related to the essential management transformation of state-owned assets in China. Holders of non-tradable shares have no incentives to enhance share value, as they cannot benefit from appreciation of share prices (Jiang & Kim, 2015; Li et al., 2011). The reform aimed to address this problem of conflicting interests between holders of tradable shares and non-tradable shares. In order to mitigate the dilution of value of tradable shares through this measure, holders of non-tradable shares needed to negotiate with holders of tradable shares regarding a compensation plan. As discussed earlier, state-owned shares that were non-tradable were converted to tradable shares.

A series of legal reforms were implemented subsequently after the split share reform in 2005. The Company Law and the Securities Law were introduced in 2006. They provide the foundation for drawing up and developing a corporate governance framework in China.

The Company Law (2006) was designed to standardize the organization and conduct of companies and to protect the legitimate rights and interests of companies, shareholders, and creditors. The Securities Law was designed to standardize securities issues and transactions, and protect the legitimate rights and interests of investors. Amendment VI to the Criminal Law (2006) aimed to match the amended Securities Law and Company Law, give a more complete definition of legal liabilities in the securities field, improve the laws governing the securities markets, and promote its sound development. These legal reforms suggest the government's intention to establish the legal foundation for corporate governance.

Following the completion of the reform on non-tradable shares, the CSRC launched a three-year campaign to strengthen the governance of listed companies in March 2007. During the campaign, listed companies looked into the existing problems in corporate governance and conducted thorough rectification of misappropriation of company funds by major shareholders, incomplete separation of funds and personnel between a listed company and its controlling shareholder, irregular operations of boards of directors of listed companies, shareholders' meetings and supervisory boards, and inadequate internal controls. These practices were not uncommon in listed companies in China.

The Law on the State-Owned Assets of Enterprises was enforced in 2009 to strengthen the country's economic system, consolidate and develop the state-owned sector, allow the state-owned enterprises to play a dominant role in the national economy, and promote the development of a socialist market economy. China's central government currently owns 106 companies, out of which 47 firms ranked in the 2014 Fortune Global 500. These centrally owned firms, or *yangqi*, controlled more than USD 5.6 trillion in assets at the end of 2013, including more than USD 690 billion abroad (Leutert, 2016).

One of the more recent and important reform measures also covers state-owned enterprises (SOEs). Beijing was aiming to transform executive compensation at its biggest state-owned firms by cutting salaries, curbing misuse of non-salary benefits, and holding managers accountable for the performance of their firms, as part of SOE reforms. Under the plan implemented since 2015, top executives at 72 central government-owned firms, which also include major companies such as PetroChina Co. Ltd., China Petroleum & Chemical Corp. (Sinopec), and China Mobile Ltd. faced pay cuts of as much as 50 percent (Reuters, 2016). Also, the government wanted to force the largest state-owned enterprises to consolidate in order to improve efficiency of those firms and to make national champions (*The Economist*, September 19, 2015). While the number of state-owned firms has decreased, the presence of state-owned firms in the economy remains significant as discussed earlier.

6.5 Board Structure

As in other countries, listed firms in China are required to have a board, and the requirements on board size and composition are stipulated in law as discussed earlier. Table 15 shows the board size and the numbers and ratios of independent directors in listed firms from 2012 to 2016. It shows that there has not been much change in terms of board size and composition in the past five years. Efficacy of independent directors is much debated as

Table 15 Board Size and Structure of Listed Firms in China

Year	Mean board size	Mean no. of independent directors	Mean percentage of independent directors (%)
2012	8.98	3.29	37.0
2013	8.86	3.27	37.4
2014	8.70	3.20	37.3
2015	8.58	3.18	37.3
2016	8.60	3.18	37.0

Source: CSMAR

most firms simply maintain the minimum required ratio of independence (Jiang & Kim, 2015), and independent directors may not have strong incentives to monitor and uphold high governance standards as they are sometimes political allies or friends of the senior executives and owners (Rajagopalan & Zhang, 2008). Nevertheless, most listed Chinese firms comply with the legal requirements.

While more than one-third of the board members are independent directors in an average Chinese listed firm, it is important to note that the primary responsibility of independent directors is to monitor large controlling shareholders (Jiang & Kim, 2015). Hence, the major focus of independent directors in China is different from that in other countries where independent directors are expected to monitor managerial decision-makings.

Table 16 shows board size and structure of the largest 20 firms in China. By looking at only the largest firms, they appear to have larger boards compared to the average listed firms. Not surprisingly, most state-owned firms have directors who are linked to the government. This appears to suggest that the government uses its board representations in state-owned enterprises to exert its influence.

Table 16 Board Structure of the Largest 20 Firms in China

Rank	Company	Board size	No. of ID	CEO-chair duality	No. of government-linked directors*
1	Tencent Holdings	8	4	Yes	–
2	Alibaba	11	5	No	–
3	ICBC	15	5	No	3
4	PetroChina	13	4	No	9
5	China Construction Bank	13	4	No	1
6	Agricultural Bank of China	14	5	No	9
7	Bank of China	13	5	No	3
8	China Petroleum & Chemical	10	4	No	2
9	China Life Insurance	14	6	No	–
10	Kweichow Moutai	14	4	No	–
11	China Merchants Bank	16	6	No	2
12	Bank of Communications	18	6	No	4
13	Baidu	8	3	Yes	–
14	Postal Savings Bank of China	12	4	No	7
15	China Shenhua Energy	7	3	No	1
16	Shanghai Pudong Development	15	6	No	–
17	JD.com	10	3	Yes	1
18	Industrial Bank	12	5	No	1
19	China Minsheng Bank	17	6	No	1
20	SAIC Motor	7	3	No	–

Source: CSMAR

* Directors who have worked or are working in government ministries and/or investing in state-owned enterprises and its subsidiaries (such as China Investment Corporation and SASAC of the State Council). Due to the high number of such enterprises under smaller Regional Governments, the number should be treated as estimate.

6.6 Shareholding Structure

Listed firms in China can be broadly categorized into two groups: state-owned enterprises and privately owned firms. Table 17 shows that there are still many firms among the largest 20 listed firms that have state ownership. This suggests that one of the primary corporate governance issues in China is the problem between

Table 17 Shareholding Structure of the Largest 20 Firms in China

Rank	Company	State ownership (%)	Institutional ownership (except for state) (%)
1	Tencent Holdings	0	5.8
2	Alibaba	0	8.4
3	ICBC	4.4	6.6
4	PetroChina	86.1	12.1
5	China Construction Bank	0.5	37.5
6	Agricultural Bank of China	44.9	47.7
7	Bank of China	7.0	4.0
8	China Petroleum & Chemical	2.8	20.8
9	China Life Insurance	92.8	3.8
10	Kweichow Moutai	64.2	8.6
11	China Merchants Bank	43.2	16.17
12	Bank of Communications	50.4	6.8
13	Baidu	0	12.2
14	Postal Savings Bank of China	49.2	13.3
15	China Shenhua Energy	88.1	4.7
16	Shanghai Pudong Development	27.6	5.4
17	JD.com	0	20.8
18	Industrial Bank	5.3	16.0
19	China Minsheng Bank	0	12.8
20	SAIC Motor	81.0	6.0

Source: Forbes 2017 (By Market Capitalization); CSMAR

dominant state owners and minority shareholders. For this reason, as discussed earlier, independent directors are responsible for monitoring large controlling shareholders, although research shows inconclusive results on the efficacy of independent board in Chinese companies (Jiang & Kim, 2015).

6.7 Executive Compensation

Total executive and director compensation in China has been rising rapidly in recent years, as shown in Table 18. Since 2007, executives and directors of state-owned enterprise have been receiving higher pay than those of non-state-owned enterprises, although executive pay at state-owned enterprises was lower before 2006. One reason for this shift is that CSRC encouraged state-owned enterprises to offer incentive mechanisms to motivate executives of those firms in 2005. This is an important issue in the Chinese context for the following reason. Executives of state-owned enterprises are usually employed by the government, and they often return to government positions after their managerial term is over. Those executives are thus motivated to gain higher government positions when they return to the government sector. Hence, even without financial incentives, they are motivated to perform well as executives. The government's push for incentive

Table 18 Annual Emolument of Top Three Executives in Chinese Firms (in CNY)

Year	Mean	Median	Max
2012	1711904	1271800	30680000
2013	1849422	1344100	32657900
2014	1962257	1425000	27137000
2015	2148320	1530450	34361840
2016	2339854	1670750	36266700

Source: CSMAR

mechanisms even for executives of state-owned firms suggests that as the government cares more about performance, including share prices and efficiency of state-owned enterprises (Jiang & Kim, 2015), it may believe that financial incentives provide further motivation to executives.

However, the government's recent reform initiatives of state-owned enterprises also negatively affected executive compensation of those firms. Chairmen and presidents of China's five biggest banks saw their 2015 compensation slashed by a record 50 percent, as the lenders' annual reports showed, after Beijing-mandated pay reforms for executives of state-owned firms were implemented. This was an effect of the SOE reformation by the new governance laws. These changes suggest that the government has a strong influence even on executive compensation, especially in state-owned enterprises.

6.8 Conclusions on Corporate Governance in China

6.8.1 Summary of Major Trends

Since the release of the corporate governance code in 2002, the government of China has implemented a series of reform measures to improve its corporate governance system for listed firms. Independent directors account for over one-third of the board in most listed Chinese firms. Executive compensation has increasingly been used to motivate executives and directors, and the pay levels have indeed risen rapidly in recent years. Shareholdings by institutional investors have also been increasing in many listed firms. Therefore, we can argue that there have been much structural improvements in corporate governance of Chinese firms.

6.8.2 Remaining Challenges

Despite the improvements being made, China is still ranked only ninth among 11 Asian economies surveyed by the Asian Corporate Governance Association (CG Watch, 2016). Although various new laws and regulations related to corporate governance have been issued, the legal system is still relatively weak in China and, consequently, investors or minority shareholders are not well protected. China is the 79 least corrupt nation out of 175 countries, according to the 2016 Corruption Perceptions Index reported by Transparency International. The report says that China has been engaging in anti-corruption efforts to catch both big and small officials who are involved with corruption, but that there is a lack of transparency and independent oversight in these efforts (Transparency International, 2017). This implies that the rule of law may not be necessarily well respected even in the fight for corruption.

Further, despite the government initiatives to reform stateowned enterprises, state ownership is still significant in many of these firms and state-owned enterprises are still inefficient. Although shareholdings of institutional investors have been increasing, it is argued that they tend to have short-term investment horizon. In emerging markets where markets are highly volatile like those in China, they are not likely to engage in monitoring their investees as they seek short-term return (Jiang & Kim, 2015). After all, as many listed Chinese firms still have controlling shareholders, it would be difficult for institutional investors to demand changes that are not acceptable to those controlling shareholders in an environment where minority shareholders are not well protected. Since those issues are inherently intertwined with China's political system, it is hard to predict how its corporate governance system will progress.

7 Taiwan

7.1 *Institutional Context*

One of the key characteristics of the corporate landscape in Taiwan is that small and medium-sized enterprises (SMEs) follow a traditional corporation style, accounting for over 90 percent of total companies. The board members in SMEs are often family-related, and many companies in Taiwan do not have a large number of outside shareholders who are not members of the family owners or business partners. It is also suggested that key business decisions are usually made at the "family board" (Securities and Futures Institute, 2007). This practice often continues even after a company goes public and lists its shares on the stock exchange. Hence, even among listed companies, family control is still prevalent and family owners continue to hold significant equity stakes.

Another characteristic in Taiwan is the presence of business groups similar to Korea. Historically, many businesses in Taiwan started from a primary industry and gradually diversified into other business segments over time, and eventually formed diversified business groups (Chung & Mahmood, 2010). The business groups often use cross-shareholding of affiliated companies to strengthen their control of listed companies, as happens in Korean chaebols. Those business group companies also rely on external finance using stocks of business group companies as collateral, which is suggested to lead to a hidden financial risk among listed companies. Financial troubles that many Taiwanese companies faced in the crisis in 1997 were the outcomes of such practice.

The Asian Financial Crisis was thus the major impetus for Taiwan to start reforming its corporate governance system, especially as weak corporate governance was identified by the international organizations as one of the key factors that led to the crisis. Since 1998, therefore, Taiwan's securities regulator (Financial Supervisory Commission or FSC) has been pushing for better corporate governance regulations and rules. Similar to many other jurisdictions, Taiwan's approach to address corporate governance issues is based on a "comply or explain" principle: regulatory bodies issue guidelines that are non-mandatory. The aim of these guidelines is to raise the public awareness of good corporate governance practices rather than to force hard-line rules by punishing companies that do not comply.

7.2   Regulatory Changes on Cross-Shareholding

Before 2001, despite some potential problems in cross-shareholding, there was no legal rule prohibiting cross-shareholding between parent and subsidiary companies or between business group companies in Taiwan's Company Law. This allowed some companies to abuse the system. For example, subsidiary companies are first established as investment companies and they then buy a large amount of their publicly listed parent companies' shares. Once the subsidiaries acquire the parent companies' shares, those subsidiary companies can be elected as directors or supervisors of the board of the parent companies, and they participate in decision-makings on the board (Securities and Futures Institute, 2007).

In order to avoid the abuse of the legal system, the 2001 amended company law which prohibits subordinate company or subsidiaries from buying any of controlling or parent company's shares. A further amendment was made to the company law in 2005, which bans a company to have any voting power for the share the company itself issued and in its own possession. Hence, a series of legal reforms has been implemented to mitigate the abuse and risk of cross-shareholding between related companies.

7.3   Recent Developments and Other Regulatory Changes

One of the major projects in recent years is the Corporate Governance Evaluation System that is to be carried out by all companies listed on the Taiwan Stock Exchange (TWSE) and the Taipei Stock Exchange (TPEx). The system was introduced in 2014, allowing investors to compare corporate governance evaluation results across companies in order for them to examine this additional dimension when they assess firm performance for their investment decisions.

A milestone in the implementation of this system was the introduction of the Corporate Governance 100 ETF Index in 2015. With this introduction, investors now have a new investment product based on the evaluation results from 2014. This is to stimulate competition among listed companies to improve their corporate governance structure and to promote investors to take the initiative in terms of demanding for fair and accountable disclosures from companies. Table 19 shows major events related to corporate governance reforms in Taiwan since the late 1990s.

Table 19 Development of Corporate Governance in Taiwan

Year	Event
1998	Promotion of corporate governance started
2002	Corporate Governance Best Practice Principles for TWSE/TPEx listed companies released
2003	Formation of Corporate Governance Task Force and the release of action plans
	Implementation of Information Disclosure and Transparency Ranking System
2006	Amendments to Company Act (2005) and Securities Exchange Act (2006)
	First phase implementation of the independent director system
2010	Amendments to Securities Exchange Act (2006). Listed companies required to asset up Remuneration Committee
2011	Second phase implementation of the independent director system
2013	Corporate Governance Roadmap announced by the FSC and the Corporate Governance Center established by the TWSE
	FSC announced that all listed companies on TWSE/TPEx to have independent directors by 2015
2015	The TWSE Corporate Governance Center released the results of the first-year evaluations of corporate governance
	The TWSE Corporate Governance 100 Index (CG100) was launched by the TWSE, and the TPEx launched its Corporate Governance Index (TPCGI)
2016	The TWSE announced the Stewardship Principles for Institutional Investors

Source: SFC

Following the release of Stewardship Codes in various countries around the world, Taiwan also released a Stewardship Code at the end of 2016 to provide guiding principles for institutional investors to fulfil their responsibilities as informed stakeholders of companies. These principles also follow a "comply or explain" approach as with other economies to allow for flexibility when fulfilling responsibilities. This is also in lieu of the fact that institutional investors are increasing their shareholdings in companies as the economy starts to remove individuals from maintaining too much control over a firm.

7.4 Board Structure

As with many Asian economies, Taiwan's first initiative to improving corporate governance of listed companies has been the introduction of independent directors. The initiative is meant to ensure the presence of oversight of executive directors of listed companies. Taiwan mandated at least two independent directors to be on each board, but this rule was soon removed and companies were allowed to nominate independent directors out of their own accord with the amendment of the Securities and Exchange Act in 2006. However, in 2013, Taiwan reintroduced mandatory independent directors for listed companies with compliance by 2017. Table 20

Table 20 Listed Companies with Independent Directors System in Taiwan

| Year | TWSE | | TPEx | |
	No. of companies	% of Total	No. of companies	% of Total
2011	369	46.7	474	78.1
2012	420	51.9	496	77.7
2013	461	55.0	528	80.2
2014	488	57.1	532	77.7
2015	638	73.0	630	88.5
2016	766	87.0	678	94.0

Source: TWSE Corporate Governance Center http://cgc.twse.com.tw/independentDr/enPage

shows the proportions of listed companies that have adopted the independent director system.

Prior to 2006, Taiwan's regulatory model of corporation followed a two-tier structure that consists of board of director, supervisor(s), and shareholders. Shareholders elect directors and supervisor(s) at a shareholder's meeting. Supervisors must clear a list of criterion of independence before they are elected. Every company must have at least two supervisors, while publicly listed firms need to have three supervisors. The function of supervisors in Taiwanese companies is similar to the audit committee in the United States and some other jurisdictions. The board of directors has discretionary power on behalf of shareholders and also performs the functions of management. Shareholders retain the power to remove a director who abuses the discretionary power that should be used to enhance shareholders' interests. Supervisor monitors directors' improper behavior and audit managerial execution by executives.

In 2006, the audit committee system was introduced as an alternative structure to the supervisory system. The audit committee system serves a similar function to the supervisors, but requires a more stringent standard regarding the composition of the committee. Each committee is to comprise of three or more independent directors, with at least one member holding an expertise in finance or accounting.

Thereafter, as part of the Corporate Governance Roadmap introduced in 2013, Taiwan has mandated that TWSE/TPEx-listed companies with capital of over TWD 2 billion to set up an audit committee by 2017 (see Table 21). The remuneration committee was also introduced in 2010 by the stock exchange to be comprised of independent directors to ensure fair compensation to board members and key executives.

Securities and Exchange Act also mentions the criteria for an independent director candidate. Specifically, the act stipulates that director candidates should meet one of the following professional

Table 21 Listed Companies with Audit Committee in Taiwan

Date	TWSE		TPEx	
	No. of companies	% of Total	No. of companies	% of Total
June 2014	159	18.8	98	14.7
December 2014	170	19.9	106	15.5
June 2015	219	25.4	134	19.2
December 2015	243	27.9	156	21.9
June 2016	306	34.7	187	25.9

Source: TWSE Corporate Governance Center http://cgc.twse.com.tw/auditCommittee/enPage

qualification requirements, in addition to at least five-year work experience:

- An instructor or higher in a department of commerce, law, finance, accounting, or other academic department related to the business needs of the company in a public or private junior college, college, or university.
- A judge, public prosecutor, attorney, certified public accountant, or other professional or technical specialist who has passed a national examination and been awarded a certificate in a profession necessary for the business of the company.
- Have work experience in the area of commerce, law, finance, or accounting, or otherwise necessary for the business of the company.

7.5   Shareholding Structure

While many companies in Taiwan are still characterized by ownership concentration, especially by family owners, there has been a trend of separation of ownership and control after Taiwanese businesses moved from labor-intensive industries to more technology-intensive industries since the early 1980s. One of the reasons given for this trend is that technology-intensive companies have to share equity ownership with other professionals such as scientists, engineers, and managers, as those companies need their skills and expertise to stay competitive (Securities and Futures Institute, 2007). Indeed, among the largest listed companies in Taiwan, many of them do not have large block holders who are insiders or family owners, as shown in Table 22.

Nevertheless, on the stock market in Taiwan, individual investors still account for almost 80 percent of trading volume. Individual investors tend to make investment decisions not based on deep company analysis but rather on market sentiment, leading to their frequent trading behavior similar to individual investors in China. Further, individual investors usually do not actively engage in voicing their views using their voting right as most of them have only small holdings, and they do not act together as a cohesive group vis-à-vis management of their investees. Therefore, it is hard to expect individual investors to play a major governance role.

As for institutional investors, they tend to play a passive role in corporate governance in Taiwan, although the government aims to increase the role of those investors. Compared to some developed countries such as the United States where institutional investors usually play a quite active role in monitoring key managerial decisions and pushing for better corporate governance in their investee companies, institutional investors do not play such a role. Hence, even though institutional ownership ratios are quite high in some large listed companies, their influence appears to be still limited. Nevertheless, the recently issued Stewardship Code aims to encourage institutional investors to play a more active corporate governance role in Taiwan.

7.6   Conclusion on Corporate Governance in Taiwan

7.6.1   Summary of Major Trends

Taiwan has been making steady progress in its corporate governance rules and regulatory framework raising required standards for listed companies as discussed earlier in this section. Almost 90 percent of listed companies in Taiwan now have independent

Table 22 Ownership Structure of the Largest 20 Companies in Taiwan

	Company Name	Institutions	Corp (private)	VC/PE	Individuals	State
1	Taiwan Semiconductor	53.0	1.0	6.4	2.4	0.0
2	Hon Hai Precision	22.5	13.4	0.0	21.6	2.2
3	Fomosa Petrochemical	2.4	0.0	0.0	0.0	0.0
4	Chunghwa Telecom	15.1	0.0	0.0	0.0	39.8
5	Cathay Financial Holdings	31.8	0.6	0.6	1.2	0.0
6	Fomosa Plastics	8.7	0.0	0.0	0.0	0.0
7	Nan Ya Plastics	7.8	0.0	0.0	0.0	0.0
8	Formosa Chemicals & Fibre	8.2	0.0	0.0	0.0	0.0
9	Fubon Financial Holdings	27.1	6.0	0.0	13.6	13.1
10	Largan Precision	30.9	0.0	0.0	0.0	0.0
11	Deta Electronics	27.2	0.0	0.0	0.0	0.0
12	China Steel	9.0	0.0	0.0	0.0	20.5
13	Taiwan Mobile Co.	20.0	0.0	0.0	0.0	0.0
14	CTBC Financial Holding	22.6	2.8	0.0	3.9	0.0
15	MediaTek	22.2	0.0	0.0	0.0	0.0
16	Mega Financial Holdings	19.9	0.4	6.1	0.7	13.3
17	Uni-President Enterprises	21.7	0.0	0.0	0.0	0.0
18	Advanced Semiconductor Engineering	25.8	26.9	0.0	58.1	0.0
19	President Chain Store	25.8	0.2	0.0	0.7	0.0
20	Far EasTone telecommunications	66.9	0.0	0.0	0.0	3.1

Source: TWSE (2016) www.twse.com.tw/ch/about/company/download/factbook/2017/1.04.html

directors and the number of companies that have an audit committee has been increasing. Formal rules that regulate abuses of cross-shareholding have also been tightened. These changes aimed to improve corporate governance in Taiwan by essentially addressing the problems of family-controlled firms and business groups. As a result, Taiwan's corporate governance is ranked fourth and only behind Singapore, Hong Kong, and Japan according to the survey by the Asian Corporate Governance Association in 2016 (CG Watch, 2016). Its governance score has especially improved in the last few years, indicating the government's strong efforts in taking initiatives.

7.6.2   Remaining Challenges

All these changes in rules and requirements suggest that Taiwan has a much stronger corporate governance framework. Yet, some remaining issues include whether many companies, especially SMEs, that are still controlled by family owners can not only comply with the governance requirements but also embrace the substance of the new rules. According to the 2016 Corruption Perceptions Index reported by Transparency International, Taiwan is the 31st least corrupt nation out of 176 countries, with a score of 61 (Transparency International, 2017). This suggests that the risk of corruption in Taiwan is relatively low compared to most other Asian countries such as China and Malaysia, indicating that the government in Taiwan is effectively enforcing rules and laws. Therefore, we expect that companies will comply with the new rules. However, family owners often seek to retain control over their firm for socioemotional reasons, and thus the strict enforcement of independence on independent directors may face some challenge. Among the different categories that constitute the corporate governance score, corporate governance culture is still relatively lower in Taiwan in the governance survey (CG Watch, 2016). This may be a reflection of family-controlled firms not showing much interest in corporate governance and still not accepting some practices such as independent chair and board evaluations. Family-controlled firms are prevalent in most Asian countries and this issue is likely not specific to Taiwan, but greater efforts are perhaps required to enhance their awareness of sound corporate governance.

8 Malaysia

8.1 *Institutional Context*

Similar to companies in other Asian countries, Malaysian companies are also characterized by concentrated ownership structure, especially by state agencies and family owners. Further, like other Asian countries, corporate governance in Malaysia started to change after the Asian Financial Crisis in 1997, although the Malaysian government did not seek financial assistance from international organizations such as IMF and the World Bank as Korea did. As a response to the crisis, the then Prime Minister Mahathir Mohamad started the National Economic Recovery Plan in 1998 with the aim of achieving market stability (Tsui-Auch, Yang, & Yoshikawa, 2016).

In line with the efforts to reform the Malaysian economy and rebuild confidence in capital markets, the Malaysian Code on Corporate Governance was issued in 2000 with recommended principles and practices as in governance codes in other countries. The Code recommends listed companies to have at least one-third board members to be independent, and the listing rules of the Kuala Lumpur Stock Exchange (KLSE) require the essentially the same practice – at least two independent directors or one-third of the board to be independent whichever is higher. One other important item in the code is that independent directors are defined as those who are independent of management and the company's major shareholder (IIF, 2006). Given high levels of ownership concentration among Malaysian companies, this was an important issue as controlling owners often use board positions, in addition to executive power, to influence key firm decisions.

While many listed companies made changes to their boards and claimed to have appointed independent directors following the

Code and the listing requirements of KLSE, it was also reported that many companies did not explain why those appointed directors can be treated as independent (World Bank, 2012) and the board often had family members and friends (Tsui-Auch et al., 2016). Yet, due to their need to attract investors, family-controlled firms were more willing to comply with the code and rules, even though those firms are mostly small and medium-sized companies. Unlike government-linked companies (GLCs) in Singapore, GLCs in Malaysia have generally shown less compliance than family-controlled companies (Tsui-Auch et al., 2016).

8.2 Recent Legal and Regulatory Changes

The Securities Commission Malaysia (SC) released the proposed draft Malaysian Code on Corporate Governance 2016 (MCCG 2016) for public consultation. The first Malaysian Code on Corporate Governance was introduced in 2000, and the code was revised twice in 2007 and 2012 with the aim of ensuring that its principles and recommendations were aligned with new business practices and market developments.

The MCCG 2016 adopts a different approach from previous corporate governance codes. The new approach has been adopted to emphasize actual conduct and outcomes from corporate governance practices. The new MCCG also places greater emphasis on the internalization of corporate governance culture, not just among listed companies, but also among non-listed entities including state-owned enterprises and small and medium-sized companies to embrace the code.

One of the key features of the new code is the introduction of the Comprehend, Apply and Report (CARE) approach and the shift from "comply or explain" to "apply or explain an alternative." The aim of this shift is to encourage listed companies to consider their corporate governance practices more seriously when they adopt and report on them. The code also identifies certain practices and reporting expectations only apply to companies in the FTSE

Bursa Malaysia Top 100 Index, and those with a market capitalization of MYR 2 billion or more. Another new aspect in the code is the introduction of "Step Up" practices to encourage companies to improve their corporate governance practices. This includes practices such as an audit committee comprised of only independent directors and the establishment of a risk management committee. Alongside the MCCG, SC also announced a three-year strategic plan to advance key corporate governance priorities as follows (source: SCM):

Strengthening the ecosystem: SC will work with stakeholders to establish the Institute of Corporate Directors Malaysia (ICDM) to provide a professional development pathway for directors. A corporate governance council will be established to coordinate all corporate governance initiatives.

Leveraging technology: SC will deploy big data and artificial intelligence capabilities to strengthen its corporate surveillance and enforcement capabilities. The SC will work with the fintech community to facilitate electronic voting and remote shareholders participation and to develop an online platform for monitoring and reporting of corporate governance practices.

Promoting gender diversity on boards: SC will collaborate with industry groups and stakeholders to increase women's participation in boards of the top 100 companies on Bursa Malaysia from 16.8 percent currently to 30 percent by 2020.

Embedding corporate governance culture early: SC will collaborate with relevant stakeholders to develop a corporate governance toolkit for SMEs to ease them into embracing good governance practices. A similar framework for licensed and registered capital market intermediaries will also be introduced. SC will also collaborate with tertiary institutions to introduce corporate governance in their curriculums to shape future corporate leaders with high ethical standards.

While these initiatives are also often proposed in other jurisdictions, they nonetheless touch on recent and fundamental issues that affect the quality of corporate governance including director training and enhancement of corporate governance culture if these initiatives go beyond symbolic moves and deeper at substantive level.

8.3   Board Recommendations in the Draft Corporate Governance Code 2016

The draft Corporate Governance Code 2016 touches on several issues related to board: board composition, independence, nomination and election, and remuneration. What the draft code says about the board composition is rather general, recommending that the board should be of sufficient size, should not be too large, and board diversity is important for board effectiveness.

The draft code raises many more points on board independence while some of them are quite general. For example, it is written that boards should be active responsible fiduciaries, no one has unfettered decision-making power, and the board has the presence of independent voice. Other issues related to board independence are as follows:

- Boards should be responsible for assessing independent directors' independence annually, upon readmission and when any new interest or relationship develops. They should disclose how the assessment was undertaken and how board independence is preserved.
- The positions of Chairman and CEO are held by different individuals, and the Chairman is a non-executive member of the board.
- The board comprises a majority of independent directors where the Chairman of the board is not an independent director.
- The board has a nine-year tenure limit for an independent director which starts from the first day of the director's appointment to the board as an independent director. Upon completion of nine years, the independent director may continue to serve on the board, subject to the director's re-designation as a non-independent director.
- In the event the board intends to retain an independent director who has served in that capacity for more than nine years, the

board seeks shareholders' approval annually through a separate resolution and provides the reasons they believe the individual remains independent and should be re-elected as an independent director.

- The board undertakes an assessment on the independence and objectivity of its independent directors annually.
- The board appoints a Senior Independent Director (SID) from the independent board members.

One of the key issues in these recommendations is that independent directors' independence to be assessed annually. Other issues such as the term limit of nine years as an independent director, the presence of independent board chair if a board does not have a majority of independent directors on the board, and the appointment of SID are increasingly adopted globally. Even after the introduction of the previous code in 2012, however, many Malaysian companies have already adopted some of the recommendations as shown below.

8.4   Changes in Board Structure

From the introduction of the code 2012 to the code 2016, the only noticeable change was the proportion of independent directors. Corporate boards that have over 50 percent of independent directors rose from 33 percent to 61 percent, while there have not been much change in CEO duality and the appointment of independent board chair, as shown in Table 23.

Table 24 shows the board structure of the 10 largest listed companies in Malaysia. Consistent with Table 23, the proportions of independent directors of large companies are generally high with some exceptions. In addition, another key feature is the presence of directors who are linked to government entities. The prevalence of government-linked directors among the country's largest companies indicates that the state's influence in the corporate sector is still significant.

Table 23 Changes in Board Structure in Malaysia

	2012	2013	2014	2015	2016
Average board size	8	8.5	8.6	8.1	8.4
CEO duality	94%	95%	95%	96%	89%
Independent board chair	40%	43%	45%	45%	41%
More than 50% IDs	33%	35%	51%	66%	61%

Source: Minority Shareholder Watchdog Group

Table 24 Board Structure of the 10 Largest Listed Firms in Malaysia

Rank	Company	Board size	No. of ID	CEO-chair duality	No. of government-linked directors*
1	Maybank	13	9	No	1
2	Tenaga Nasional	13	8	No	5
3	Public Bank	8	4	No	1
4	Sime Darby	14	4	No	6
5	Petronas Chemicals	8	4	No	0
6	Cimb Group Holdings	11	6	No	5
7	Maxis	11	4	No	0
8	Axiata Group	10	5	No	4
9	Petronas Gas	7	2	No	0
10	Genting	9	5	Yes	3

Source: Company annual reports

* Directors who have worked or are working in government ministries and/or investing state-owned enterprises (such as Khazanah Nasional Berhad, Employees Provident Fund Board and AmanahRaya)

8.5 *Shareholding Structure*

As mentioned earlier, many listed companies in Malaysia have block owners such as family owners and state agencies. Among

Table 25 Shareholding Structure of the 10 Largest Firms in Malaysia

Rank	Company	State ownership*	Institutional ownership (except for state)
1	Maybank	53.0	21.0
2	Tenaga Nasional	54.5	11.7
3	Public Bank	17.1	35.9
4	Sime Darby	68.7	9.7
5	Petronas Chemicals	82.2	5.3
6	Cimb Group Holdings	56.6	13.7
7	Maxis	21.7	69.9
8	Axiata Group	73.5	8.0
9	Petronas Gas	84.6	4.3
10	Genting	0	66.4

Source: Company annual reports Market capitalization based on 2016 data
* Khazanah Nasional Berhad, Employees Provident Fund Board, AmanahRaya

the largest companies, large shareholders tend to be mostly state owners. Table 25 shows ownership stakes by state agencies and institutional investors in the largest 10 companies in Malaysia. As consistent with the presence of government-linked directors in most of those companies, the state has a significant ownership of power in the largest companies in the country.

One of the important implications of this characteristic is that the state's role of large shareholders and regulator can create conflicts of interest (Gomez, 2012), which may damage the interests of minority shareholders in some situations. It was argued that the state's conflicting roles may have been a cause of frequent scandals involving state-owned corporations in Malaysia where the state as a regulator is responsible for monitoring corporate misdeeds, and yet the state is often involved on the board and as executives of those companies (Tsui-Auch et al., 2016). Hence, the state's large presence as shareholders in large listed companies can create tensions when the corporate governance standards need to be improved.

8.6 Conclusion on Corporate Governance in Malaysia

8.6.1 Summary of Major Trends

Since the introduction of the first code in 2000, corporate governance rules in Malaysia have been improving with a series of revisions on the code. Now many corporate boards of listed Malaysian companies have at least one-third and many have a majority of independent directors on their boards. Many companies have also separated CEO and board chair positions. The proposed draft corporate governance code aims to improve the existing rules by more strictly assessing independence of independent directors.

Despite all these improvements in rules related to corporate governance, many large listed companies are still characterized by ownership concentration, especially by state owners, and indeed many boards have government-linked directors. As discussed earlier, the dual role of the state may be creating tensions, and Malaysia's corporate governance ranking as 6th out of 11 Asian countries, based on the survey by Asian Corporate Governance Association (CG Watch, 2016), may be attributed to this. It ranks above Korea and China but tails Singapore, Japan, and Taiwan.

8.6.2 Remaining Challenges

If we look at the dimensions of corporate governance assessed by this survey, political and regulatory environments especially have low scores. This category includes such factors as political support for corporate governance reforms, the quality of the judiciary, the presence of anti-corruption agency, and the government's protection of civil service ethics (CG Watch, 2016). As scandals involving government-linked corporations and senior politicians are frequent, corruption still seems to be affecting this category in the assessment of corporate governance of Malaysia. Malaysia is 55th least corrupt nation out of 175 countries, according to the 2016 Corruption Perceptions Index reported by Transparency International. This ranking is still better than China but far worse than Singapore, Japan, and Taiwan.

In addition, corporate governance culture is another category in this ranking where Malaysia is relatively weak. It is suggested that the ability of boards with independent directors to effectively monitor the management of Malaysian companies is often questioned (Tsui-Auch et al., 2016). The SC's one of the strategic initiatives is to embed corporate governance culture early among SMEs. Whether it can successfully establish strong corporate governance culture also depends on whether political and regulatory environments, as public governance remains an issue, would affect how frequent occurrence of scandals involving government-linked corporations can be addressed.

9   Discussion and Conclusions

9.1   Summary and Discussion

This Element has reviewed and discussed the key characteristics, recent trends, and some challenges in corporate governance in Japan, Singapore, Korea, China, Taiwan, and Malaysia. They include various economies at different levels of economic development and the three largest economies in East Asia, i.e., China, Japan, and Korea. Although these economies are at different levels of economic development, one common factor is that most of them started to reform their corporate governance rules and systems after the Asian Financial Crisis. About 20 years since the crisis, all these economies have made significant changes to their rules and regulations related to corporate governance, and the board structure and other practices such as information disclosure and executive compensation have also changed and become more transparent and appear more accountable. Yet, there are still many differences in terms of the degree and directions of changes among those economies.

Corporate governance reforms in Japan have accelerated since Prime Minister Abe has started to push for such changes as part of the economic revitalization plan. In the past, large Japanese companies were dragging their feet on major changes that may affect their top decision-making structure (i.e., board). However, the strong government initiative has made listed Japanese companies to include independent directors, and the number of such directors has been increasing especially among the largest companies. Institutional investors along with the proxy advisory firms are also demanding Japanese companies to increase qualified independent directors on boards. Hence, Japanese boards have gone through significant changes in the last few years. One remaining issue is how far Japanese corporate governance will continue to change as they started from a relatively low base; still most Japanese boards do not have a majority of independent directors.

Singapore continues to maintain high corporate governance standards and is continually updating the requirements. Most of large listed companies have a majority of independent directors on their boards, and the requirements on independence have been becoming stricter. However, like many other Asian economies, for many listed companies especially for family-owned SMEs, keeping high corporate governance standards is costly. Further, many companies have concentrated ownership, which may stifle pressures from outside investors. Hence, strong commitment by the government and regulatory body is a key factor in maintaining its high governance ranking in Asia.

Korea also has made significant changes to its corporate governance system after the Asian Financial Crisis. However, the Korean economy has been heavily influenced by chaebols, and the government has not been able to restructure its economy by reforming corporate governance of those family-controlled business groups. The recent change in the political leadership and the reported exposure of the close relationship between the President and chaebol may reignite the initiative to reform business groups, some of which have been resisting governance reforms.

China has implemented a series of corporate governance reform measures and the current formal requirements – for example, on board composition – are comparable to other economies. At the same time, the government has been trying to reform state-owned enterprises that are highly inefficient. However, even with improved corporate governance standards and decreasing presence of state-owned enterprises, governmental control to promote national interests is still highly visible and the power of institutional investors is still rather limited. A remaining challenge is thus how to reconcile these tensions.

Taiwan is also characterized by ownership concentration and the prevalence of family-controlled companies. In those companies, it is common that family owners and managers make key corporate decisions without much transparency. However, corporate governance rules and regulations have become much stronger over years and their standards have been improving. The regulatory body is also trying to enhance awareness and competition among listed companies to improve their corporate governance, for example, by introducing the corporate governance index which investors can use to assess their invested companies' governance practices. One of the remaining issues would be to further enhance corporate governance culture, especially among family-controlled SMEs.

Similar to other Asian economies, Malaysia has also improved its corporate governance standards, and now most listed companies have over one-third of their board members who are independent, and the separation of CEO and board chair is becoming common. At the same time, large companies in Malaysia are characterized by the presence of large state owners, while smaller firms are often controlled by family owners. Further, public governance involving scandals of politicians and state-owned entities are frequent. These issues require improvement in corporate governance culture and in regulatory and political environments. This means that challenges are not merely in governance-related rules and regulations but in the institutional environments in which corporate governance system and companies are embedded.

9.2 Implications

Based on the standard measures, corporate governance in Asian economies has been generally improving, especially board structure and transparency. Most boards in Asian companies were dominated by insiders including representatives of controlling owners, family members, and insider executives in the past, but they now have independent directors although at various levels. Two financial centers, i.e., Singapore and Hong Kong, are leading in corporate governance reforms, and some others are closely following them, while some economies are rather stagnant in reforms. Although corporate governance rules and regulations are in place and still improving in most economies, corporate governance culture remains relatively weak in some, which suggests that many changes may be still symbolic or only in form especially in the lower ranked economies in corporate governance.

Key reasons for the remaining variation among Asian economies may be due to vast differences in ownership structure (concentration of state or family owners and the identity of those owners) as well as different legal environments including the enforcement that exist among Asian economies. While most companies in the region are characterized by ownership concentration, the identity of large owners varies and the relationship between such owners and political elites varies as well by country or economy. This implies that key governance issues in each economy are different and, hence, one standard model that fit across different economies may not exist. As corporate governance is embedded in a larger institutional context, we need to pay attention not only to government policy and formal rules related to corporate governance but also to other factors such as the political culture and system, corporate culture, managerial discretionary power, and ownership structure as a bundle of corporate governance mechanisms (Aguilera, Desender, & Kabbach de Castro, 2011).

However, corporate governance debate and discussion continues to focus on the US model and the application of that model in other institutional contexts, but its model may not be applicable, for example, to family firms that are prevalent in the Asian context. The role of the board of directors may go beyond monitoring management in family firms, but may also include the maintenance of family relationships and wealth or balancing the interests of key stakeholders (Yoshikawa, Zhu, & Wang, 2014). The role of the board of directors also varies depending upon the family ownership stake, the presence of family executives, and the presence or absence of other governance mechanisms. In well-run family controlled firms, the board with many independent directors may not be always necessary or even effective when there are good regulations (e.g., on disclosure) in place in an institutional context.

Furthermore, many Asian companies (e.g., in China, Malaysia, and Singapore) are controlled by state owners. This creates other governance problems as state-owned companies are often expected to achieve some strategic goals that are consistent with national interests, which may lead to inefficiency and even exploitation of minority shareholders. Yet, state-owned firms are not monolithic entities across different countries and are not always inefficient. Depending on the relationship between the state and its investment arms as well as how such investment firms are governed, they may be able to effectively monitor their investees such as GLCs in Singapore. They sometimes have better corporate governance practices with other complimentary mechanisms (e.g., high levels of transparency). However, some countries lack an effective bundle of governance (e.g., China – ownership concentration, lack of transparency, ineffective legal enforcement). This again raises an issue of corporate governance bundle.

Corporate governance in Asia has evolved substantially since the Asian Financial Crisis but the trajectory varies by economy. We can observe consistent improvements in some economies such as in

Singapore and accelerated changes in Japan, while enforcement remains an issue in other economies such as in China. While the overall directions of corporate governance reforms appear to be similar, priorities are perhaps different by economy as each has a unique institutional environment. A further investigation of corporate governance bundles across the different Asian countries should inform us of the effectiveness of the overall system.

References

Aguilera, R.V., Desender, K.A., & Kabbach de Castro, L.R. 2011. A Configurational Approach to Comparative Corporate Governance. In T. Clarke & D. Branson (eds.). *The Sage Handbook of Corporate Governance*. New York: Sage Publications, 380–405.

Ahmadjian, C.L. & Robinson, P. 2001. Safety in numbers: Downsizing and the deinstitutionalization of permanent employment in Japan. *Administrative Science Quarterly*, 46: 622–654.

Ahmadjian, C.L. & Son, J. 2004. *Corporate Governance Reform in Japan and South Korea: Two Paths of Globalization*. Discussion Paper Series, APEC Study Center, Columbia Business School.

Aoki, M., Jackson, G., & Miyajima, H. 2007. *Corporate Governance in Japan: Institutional Change and Organizational Diversity*. Oxford, UK: Oxford University Press.

Charkham, J. 1994. *Keeping Good Company: A Study of Corporate Governance in Five Countries*. Oxford: Clarendon Press.

Chen, C.C.J. 2016. *Solving the Puzzle of Corporate Governance of State-owned Enterprises: The Path of Temasek Model in Singapore and Lessons for China*. Singapore Management University, Research Collection School of Law.

Chiang, L. 2008. China gives state firms $8 billion to combat slowdown. *Reuters*. Retrieved 22 May 2017 from www.reuters.com/article/sppage024-pek162453-oisnr-idUSPEK1624532008112.

Chizema, A. & Kim, J. 2010. Outside directors on Korean boards: Governance and institutions. *Journal of Management Studies*, 47: 109–129.

Choi, J.J., Park, S.W., & Yoo, S.S. 2007. The value of outside directors: Evidence from corporate governance reform in Korea. *Journal of Financial and Quantitative Analysis*, 42: 941–962.

Chung, C.N. & Mahmood, I.P. 2010. Business Groups in Taiwan. In A.M. Colpan, J. Lincoln, & T. Hikino (eds.). *The Oxford Handbook of Business Groups*. Oxford, UK: Oxford University Press.

CLSA and ACGA. 2007. *CG Watch 2007: Corporate Governance in Asia.* Hong Kong: Credit Lyonnais Securities Asia, Asian Corporate Governance Association.

CLSA and ACGA. 2010. *CG Watch 2010: Corporate Governance in Asia.* Hong Kong: Credit Lyonnais Securities Asia, Asian Corporate Governance Association.

CLSA and ACGA. 2012. *CG Watch 2012: Corporate Governance in Asia.* Hong Kong: Credit Lyonnais Securities Asia, Asian Corporate Governance Association.

CLSA and ACGA. 2014. *CG Watch 2014: Corporate Governance in Asia.* Hong Kong: Credit Lyonnais Securities Asia, Asian Corporate Governance Association.

CLSA and ACGA. 2016. *CG Watch 2016: Ecosystems Matter, Asia's Path to Better Home-grown Governance.* Hong Kong: Credit Lyonnais Securities Asia, Asian Corporate Governance Association.

Colpan, A.M. & Yoshikawa, T. 2012. Performance sensitivity of executive pay: The role of foreign investors and affiliated directors in Japan. *Corporate Governance: An International Review*, 20: 547–561.

Crossland, C. & Hambrick, D.C. 2011. Differences in managerial discretion across countries: How nation-level institutions affect the degree to which CEOs matter. *Strategic Management Journal*, 32: 797–819.

Daiwa Research Institute. 2017. Consulting insight, points on 2017 June general shareholders' meeting. April 26.

David, P., O'Brien, J.P., Yoshikawa, T., & Delios, A. 2010. Do shareholders or stakeholders appropriate the rents from corporate diversification? The influence of ownership structure. *Academy of Management Journal*, 53: 636–654.

Economist Intelligence Unit and Andersen Consulting. 2000. Beyond the Bamboo Network: Successful Strategies for Change in Asia. Hong Kong, China: Economist Intelligence Unit.

Ethical Boardroom. 2017. *Corporate Governance in Japan Now.* Retrieved from Ethical Boardroom: https://ethicalboardroom.com/corporate-governance-in-japan-now/. 22 March.

EY. 2012. Revised Code of Corporate Governance. Retrieved 2 May 2017 from www.ey.com/sg/en/services/assurance/board-matters-quarterly-issue-12-june-2012-revised-code-of-corporate-governance.

Fich, E.M. & Shivdasani, A. 2006. Are busy boards effective monitors? *The Journal of Finance*, 61: 689–724.

Financial Services Agency. 2014. *Principles for responsible institutional investors*. Retrieved from www.fsa.go.jp/en/refer/councils/steward ship/20140407/01.pdf. 26 February.

Forbes. 2017. The world's biggest public companies. Retrieved 31 May 2017 from www.forbes.com/global2000/list/.

Gedajlovic, E. & Shapiro, D.M. 2002. Ownership structure and firm profitability in Japan. *Academy of Management Journal*, 45: 565–575.

Geng, X., Yoshikawa, T., & Colpan, A.M. 2016. Leveraging foreign institutional logic in the adoption of stock option pay among Japanese firms. *Strategic Management Journal*, 37: 1472–1492.

Gerlach, M.L. 1992. *Alliance Capitalism: The Social Organizations of Japanese Business*. Berkeley, CA: University of California Press.

Gomez, E.T. 2012. State-Business Linkages in Southeast Asia: The Development State, Neo-Liberalism, and Enterprise Development. In A. Walter & X. Zhang (eds.). *East Asian Capitalism: Diversity, Continuity and Change*. Oxford, UK: Oxford University Press, 68–88.

Goswami, S. 2017. Study finds India is Asia's most corrupt country, while Japan comes in last. Retrieved from *Forbes*: www.forbes.com/sites/suparnagoswami/2017/03/08/study-finds-india-is-asias-most-corrupt-country-while-japan-comes-in-last/#5b3876c81201. 8 March.

Gourevitch, P. & Shinn, J.J. 2005. *Political Power and Corporate control: The New Global Politics of Corporate Governance*. Princeton: Princeton University Press.

Hamilton-Hart, N. 2002. *Asian States, Asian Bankers: Central Banking in Southeast Asia*. New York: Cornell University Press.

Hay Group. 2013. Retrieved 2 May 2017 from www.haygroup.com/downloads/sg/Hay%20Group%20Top%20Exec%20SG%20press%20release_Feb%202013.pdf.

Hay Group. 2014. Retrieved 2 May 2017 from www.haygroup.com/down loads/sg/Singapore%20CEO%20pay%20shows%20flat%20trend%20while%20company%20profitability%20dipsv2.pdf.

IIF. 2006. *Corporate Governance in Malaysia: An Investor Perspective*. The Institute of International Finance, Inc.

ISCA. 2014. Singapore directorship report. Retrieved 2 May 2017 from https://isca.org.sg/media/776653/sg-directorship-report.pdf.

ISCA. 2016. SID-ISCA Singapore Directorship Report 2016: More boards have greater proportion of independent directors (IDs) and increase in lead IDs. Retrieved 2 May 2017 from www.isca.org.sg/the-institute/newsroom/media-releases/2016/october/sid-isca-singapore-director ship-report-2016-more-boards-have-greater-proportion-of-indepen dent-directors-ids-and-increase-in-lead-ids/.

Jiang, F. & Kim, K.A. 2015. Corporate governance in China: A modern perspective. *Journal of Corporate Finance*, 32: 190–216.

Kim, H. & Lee, J.H. 2012. Transformation of Corporate Governance in Korea. In A.A. Rasheed & T. Yoshikawa (eds.). *The Convergence of Corporate Governance: Promise and Prospects*. Basingstoke: Palgrave Macmillan, 137–168.

Kim, S.Y., Lee, K.R., & Shin, H.-H. 2017. The enhanced disclosure of executive compensation in Korean. *Pacific-Basin Finance Journal*, 43: 72–83.

Leong, C.H. 2016. The Motley Fool. Retrieved 2 May 2017 from www.fool.sg/2016/07/14/how-have-government-linked-companies-in-singa pores-stock-market-fared/. 14 July.

Leutert, W. 2016. Challenges ahead in China's reform of SOE. *Asia Policy*, 21: 83–99. The National Bureau of Asian Research, Seattle, Washington.

Li, K., Wang, T., Cheung, C-L., & Jiang, P. 2011. Privatization and risk sharing: Evidence from the split share structure reform in China. *Review of Financial Studies*, 24: 2499–2525.

Minority Shareholder Watchdog Group. 2016. Key corporate governance statistics of public listed companies in Malaysia. Retrieved 5 June 2017 from www.mswg.org.my/key-corporate-governance-statistics-of-public-listed-companies-in-malaysia

Miwa, Y. & Ramseyer, J.M. 2005. Who appoints them, what do they do? Evidence on outside directors from Japan. *Journal of Economics and Management Strategy*, 14: 299–337.

Monetary Authority of Singapore. 2017. MAS announces establishment of Corporate Governance Council to review the Code of Corporate Governance. Retrieved 2 May 2017 from www.mas.gov.sg/News-and-Publications/Media-Releases/2017/MAS-Announces-Establishment-of-Corporate-Governance-Council.aspx

National University of Singapore. 2015. Ranking of the 100 largest Singapore listed companies by market capitalisation based on the ASEAN Corporate Governance Scorecard (ACGS). Retrieved 2 May 2017 from https://bschool.nus.edu/Portals/0/docs/CGIO/acgs-2015-sg-100cos.pdf

National University of Singapore. 2015. Governance of government-linked companies in Singapore. Retrieved 2 May 2017 from http://law.nus.edu.sg/clb/events/EACG_Dialogue_Conference2015/pdfs/mak_gglcs_slides.pdf.

OECD. 2004. *OECD economic survey: Korea 2004*. New York: OECD Publishing.

Oh, D. & Ahn, S.A. 2015. Retrieved from *International Law Financial Review*: www.iflr.com/Article/3429769/Improving-South-Korean-corporate-governance.html. February 25.

Phan, P.H. & Yoshikawa, T. 2004. *Corporate Governance in Singapore: Developments and Prognoses*. Paper presented at the Academy of International Business Annual Meeting, Stockholm.

Prowse, S. 1998. *Corporate Governance: Emerging Issues and Lessons from East Asia*. Washington, DC: World Bank.

Rajagopalan, N. & Zhang, Y. 2008. Corporate governance reforms in China and India: Challenges and opportunities. *Business Horizons*, 51: 55–64.

Reuters. 2016. China bank chiefs' already low pay cut in half even as problems mount. April 5. http://www.reuters.com/article/china-banks-pay/update-2

Sakamoto, M. & Harima, Y. 2014. Companies Act Reform 2014. Retrieved from City Yuwa Partners: www.city-yuwa.com/english/publication/shared/PDF/JLG201415_cy_56-59.pdf

SASAC. 2017. Central Enterprises Directory. Retrieved 22 May 2017 from www.sasac.gov.cn/n86114/n86137/index.html

Securities and Futures Institute. 2007. *Corporate Governance in Taiwan*. Taipei, May.

Securities Commission Malaysia. 2016. SC releases new Malaysian Code on Corporate Governance to strengthen corporate culture. Retrieved 5 June 2017 from www.sc.com.my/post_archive/sc-releases-new-malaysian-code-on-corporate-governance-to-strengthen-corporate-culture/

Securities Commission Malaysia. 2016. Corporate governance. Retrieved 5 June 2017 from www.sc.com.my/general-section/corporate-governance/

Sheard, P. 1994. Interlocking Shareholdings and Corporate Governance. In M. Aoki & R. Dore (eds.). *The Japanese Firm: The Sources of Competitive Strength*. Oxford, UK: Oxford University Press, 310–349.

Tan, L.H., Tan, C.T., & Ching, L.H. 2006. *Corporate Governance of Listed Companies in Singapore*. Singapore: Sweet & Maxwell Asia.

Temasek Holdings. 2016. Temasek review 2016. Retrieved 2 May 2017 from www.temasekreview.com.sg/overview/portfolio-highlights.html

The Economist. 2015. China's state-owned enterprises: A winper, not a bang. *The Economist,* September 19.

Tokyo Stock Exchange. 2015. TSE-listed companies white paper on corporate governance. Tokyo.

Tokyo Stock Exchange. 2015. TSE-listed companies white paper on corporate governance. Tokyo.

Tokyo Stock Exchange. 2015. *Japan's Corporate Governance Code.* Retrieved from www.jpx.co.jp/english/equities/listing/cg/tvdivq0000008jdy-att/20150513.pdf.

Transparency Korea Chapter. 2017. Retrieved from Transparency Korea chapter: www.transparency-korea.org/2017/01/corruption-perceptions-index-cpi-2016/

Tsui-Auch, L.S., Yang, J.J., & Yoshikawa, T. 2016. Change and Continuity in Corporate Governance Structures: A Study of Korea, Malaysia and Singapore. In R. Whitley & X. Zhang (eds.). *Changing Asian Business System.* Oxford, UK: Oxford University Press, 209–228.

Tsui-Auch, L.S. & Yoshikawa, T. 2010. Business Groups in Singapore. In A. Colpan, T. Hikino, & J. Lincoln (eds.). *The Oxford Handbook of Business Groups.* Oxford, UK: Oxford University Press, 267–293.

Tsui-Auch, L.S. & Yoshikawa, T. 2015. Institutional change versus resilience: A study of incorporation of independent directors in Singapore banks. *Asian Business & Management,* 14: 91–115.

Williams, A. 2015. *The Straits Times.* Retrieved 2 May 2017 from www.straitstimes.com/business/singapore-still-the-highest-for-executive-pay-in-asia-but-hong-kong-catching-up-survey. 12 March.

World Bank. 2012. *Malaysia – Report on the Observance of Standards and Codes (ROSC): Corporate Governance Country Assessment.* Washington, DC: World Bank.

Xiang, C.H. 2016. Proportion of IDs on boards of listed firms on the rise: Study. *Business Times.* Retrieved 2 May 2017 from www.businesstimes.com.sg/companies-markets/proportion-of-ids-on-boards-of-listed-firms-on-the-rise-study.

Yoshikawa, T. 2010. The Case of Singapore. In F.J.L. Iturriaga (ed.). *Codes of Good Governance Around the World.* Hauppauge, NY: Nova Science Publishers, 543–554.

Yoshikawa, T. & Rasheed, A. 2009. Convergence of corporate governance: Critical review and future directions. *Corporate Governance: An International Review*, 17: 388–404.

Yoshikawa, T., Zhu, H., & Wang, P. 2014. National governance system, corporate ownership, and roles of outside directors: A corporate governance bundle perspective. *Corporate Governance: An International Review*, 22: 252–265.

Printed in the United States
By Bookmasters